SPECTRUM

Fractions

Grade 6

Spectrum®
An imprint of Carson-Dellosa Publishing LLC
P.O. Box 35665
Greensboro, NC 27425 USA

© 2014 Carson-Dellosa Publishing LLC. Except as permitted under the United States Copyright Act, no part of this publication may be reproduced, stored, or distributed in any form or by any means (mechanically, electronically, recording, etc.) without the prior written consent of Carson-Dellosa Publishing LLC. Spectrum® is an imprint of Carson-Dellosa Publishing LLC.

Printed in the USA • All rights reserved.   ISBN 978-1-4838-0480-4

Table of Contents — Grade 6

Introduction 4

Chapter 1 Understanding Fractions
Chapter 1 Pretest 5–6
Practice Pages 7–14
Chapter 1 Posttest 15–16

Chapter 2 Problem Solving: Understanding Fractions
Chapter 2 Pretest 17
Practice Pages 18–24
Chapter 2 Posttest 25

Chapter 3 Adding and Subtracting Fractions
Chapter 3 Pretest 26
Practice Pages 27–33
Chapter 3 Posttest 34

Chapter 4 Problem Solving: Adding and Subtracting Fractions
Chapter 4 Pretest 35
Practice Pages 36–41
Chapter 4 Posttest 42

Mid-Test Chapters 1–4 43–44

Chapter 5 Multiplying and Dividing Fractions
Chapter 5 Pretest 45
Practice Pages 46–59
Chapter 5 Posttest 60

Chapter 6 Problem Solving: Multiplying and Dividing Fractions
Chapter 6 Pretest 61
Practice Pages 62–67
Chapter 6 Posttest 68

Chapter 7 Fractions and Decimals
Chapter 7 Pretest 69
Practice Pages 70–75
Chapter 7 Posttest 76

Final Test Chapters 1–7 77–82

Scoring Record for Pretests, Posttests, Mid-Test, and Final Test 83

Answer Key 84–96

Introduction   Grade 6

Spectrum Fractions is designed to build on the foundation for fractions laid in the fifth grade and further challenge your sixth grader. Aligned to the fifth and sixth grade Common Core State Standards for fractions, every page equips your child with the confidence to master fractions. Helpful examples provide step-by-step guidance to teach new concepts, followed by a variety of practice pages that will sharpen your child's skills and efficiency at problem solving. Use the Pretests, Posttests, Mid-Test, and Final Test as the perfect way to track your child's progress and identify where he or she needs extra practice.

Common Core State Standards Alignment: Fractions Grades 5 and 6

Domain: Number and Operations—Fractions	
Standard	Aligned Practice Pages
5.NF.1	26, 29–34, 43, 78–79
5.NF.2	35–42, 44, 80
5.NF.4a	45, 48, 52, 60
5.NF.6	45–52, 59–64, 68, 78–82
5.NF.7a	45, 54, 58–60
5.NF.7b	45, 54, 58–60
5.NF.7c	61, 66, 68, 81–82
Domain: The Number System	
Standard	Aligned Practice Pages
6.NS.1	45, 55, 58–60, 61, 65, 68, 78–79
6.NS.4	5, 8–9, 11, 15, 17, 19, 20, 24, 25, 43, 77

* © Copyright 2010. National Governors Association Center for Best Practices and Council of Chief State School Officers. All rights reserved.

Check What You Know

Understanding Fractions

Identify each number as prime (p) or composite (c).

a	b	c	d	e
1. 5 _____	8 _____	2 _____	15 _____	19 _____

Find the greatest common factor of the two numbers.

2. 8 and 12   5 and 3   24 and 36   14 and 36   15 and 75

_____   _____   _____   _____   _____

Change each fraction to its simplest form.

3. $\frac{15}{25}$ _____ $\frac{24}{36}$ _____ $\frac{25}{40}$ _____ $\frac{9}{12}$ _____ $\frac{14}{16}$ _____

Rename each pair of fractions with common denominators.

4. $\frac{3}{8}$ and $\frac{5}{12}$ $\frac{2}{3}$ and $\frac{3}{4}$ $\frac{1}{4}$ and $\frac{5}{6}$ $\frac{4}{5}$ and $\frac{1}{2}$ $\frac{2}{3}$ and $\frac{5}{7}$

_____   _____   _____   _____   _____

Check What You Know

Understanding Fractions

Change each improper fraction to a mixed numeral.

a	b	c	d	e
5. $\frac{27}{5}$ _____	$\frac{35}{8}$ _____	$\frac{15}{7}$ _____	$\frac{25}{4}$ _____	$\frac{17}{3}$ _____

Change each mixed numeral to an improper fraction.

6. $3\frac{5}{16}$ _____ $3\frac{3}{5}$ _____ $3\frac{3}{7}$ _____ $3\frac{3}{16}$ _____ $3\frac{1}{3}$ _____

Change each mixed numeral to its simplest form.

7. $3\frac{11}{3}$ _____ $5\frac{8}{10}$ _____ $1\frac{7}{5}$ _____ $3\frac{15}{18}$ _____ $4\frac{5}{4}$ _____

Prime and Composite Numbers

SCORE /8

A **prime number** is any number greater than 1 that has only two factors, itself and 1. (Ex: 2, 3, 5, 7)

A **composite number** has more than two factors. (Ex: 4 has 3 factors: 1, 2, and 4.)

A composite number can be written as a product of prime numbers. This is called the **prime factorization** of the number. A **factor tree** is used to determine the prime factorization of the number.

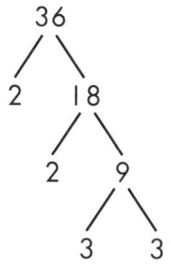

Choose any two factors to begin. Stop when all factors are prime numbers.

List the factors from smallest to largest.

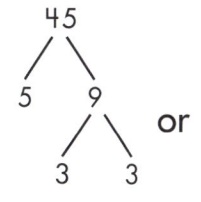 or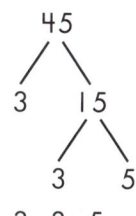

2, 2, 3, 3 is the prime factorization of 36.

Identify each number as prime (p) or composite (c).

	a	b	c
1.	6 _____	7 _____	13 _____
2.	19 _____	15 _____	8 _____

Use a factor tree to find the prime factorization of each number.

	a	b
3.	18	40

Spectrum Fractions
Grade 6

Chapter 1
Understanding Fractions

NAME _____

Finding the Greatest Common Factor

A **factor** is a divisor of a number. (For example, 3 and 4 are both factors of 12.) A **common factor** is a divisor that is shared by two or more numbers (1, 2, 4, and 8). The **greatest common factor** is the largest common factor shared by the numbers (8).

To find the greatest common factor of 32 and 40, list all of the factors of each.

$$32 \begin{cases} 1 \times 32 \\ 2 \times 16 \\ 4 \times 8 \end{cases} \quad 1, 2, 4, 8, 16, \text{ and } 32 \qquad 40 \begin{cases} 1 \times 40 \\ 2 \times 20 \\ 4 \times 10 \\ 5 \times 8 \end{cases} \quad 1, 2, 4, 5, 8, 10, 20, \text{ and } 40$$

The greatest common factor is 8.

List the factors of each number below. Then, list the common factors and the greatest common factor.

Factors   **Common Factors**   **Greatest Common Factor**

1. 8 _____   _____   _____

    12 _____

2. 6 _____   _____   _____

    18 _____

3. 24 _____   _____   _____

    15 _____

4. 4 _____   _____   _____

    6 _____

Spectrum Fractions
Grade 6

Chapter 1
Understanding Fractions

Finding the Greatest Common Factor

List the factors of each number below. Then, list the common factors and the greatest common factor.

	Factors	Common Factors	Greatest Common Factor
1. 5			
12			
2. 16			
12			
3. 15			
18			
4. 7			
3			
5. 24			
36			
6. 18			
20			

Spectrum Fractions
Grade 6

Chapter 1
Understanding Fractions

NAME _____

Reducing Fractions to Their Simplest Form

A fraction is in **simplest form** when the numerator and denominator have no common factor except 1.

$\frac{16}{24} = \frac{16 \div 8}{24 \div 8} = \frac{2}{3}$

The simplest form for $\frac{16}{24}$ is $\frac{2}{3}$.

A mixed numeral is in simplest form when its fraction is in simplest form and names a number less than 1.

$2\frac{8}{10} = 2 + \frac{8 \div 2}{10 \div 2}$

$= 2 + \frac{4}{5}$

$= 2\frac{4}{5}$

The simplest form of $2\frac{8}{10}$ is $2\frac{4}{5}$.

Change each of the following to simplest form.

      a   **b**   **c**

1. $\frac{8}{12}$ _____ $\frac{9}{24}$ _____ $\frac{10}{16}$ _____

2. $3\frac{4}{6}$ _____ $5\frac{8}{16}$ _____ $4\frac{12}{16}$ _____

3. $\frac{14}{16}$ _____ $\frac{10}{12}$ _____ $\frac{16}{40}$ _____

4. $\frac{8}{30}$ _____ $\frac{21}{36}$ _____ $\frac{15}{18}$ _____

Spectrum Fractions
Grade 6

NAME _____

SCORE ◯ /12

Finding Common Denominators

The two fractions $\frac{1}{5}$ and $\frac{3}{5}$ have common denominators. However, $\frac{1}{4}$ and $\frac{3}{5}$ do not have common denominators. Rename these fractions so that they have common denominators by finding the least common multiple of their denominators. The **least common multiple** of two numbers is the smallest number that is a multiple of both.

Multiples of 4 are 4, 8, 12, 16, 20, 24, . . .

Multiples of 5 are 5, 10, 15, 20, . . .

The smallest number that is a multiple of 4 and 5 is 20.

Rename each fraction with a denominator of 20.

$\frac{1}{4} = \frac{1 \times 5}{4 \times 5} = \frac{5}{20}$; $\frac{3}{5} = \frac{3 \times 4}{5 \times 4} = \frac{12}{20}$

$\frac{5}{20}$ and $\frac{12}{20}$ have common denominators.

Rename each pair of fractions with common denominators.

	a	b	c
1.	$\frac{1}{4}$ and $\frac{2}{3}$ _____	$\frac{3}{8}$ and $\frac{7}{10}$ _____	$\frac{4}{7}$ and $\frac{2}{3}$ _____
2.	$\frac{3}{8}$ and $\frac{1}{6}$ _____	$\frac{2}{3}$ and $\frac{1}{2}$ _____	$\frac{3}{8}$ and $\frac{5}{6}$ _____
3.	$\frac{2}{5}$ and $\frac{1}{3}$ _____	$\frac{5}{16}$ and $\frac{3}{8}$ _____	$\frac{1}{2}$ and $\frac{1}{3}$ _____
4.	$\frac{5}{8}$ and $\frac{3}{16}$ _____	$\frac{2}{5}$ and $\frac{3}{4}$ _____	$\frac{5}{12}$ and $\frac{4}{5}$ _____

Spectrum Fractions
Grade 6

Chapter 1
Understanding Fractions

NAME _____

Changing Improper Fractions to Mixed Numerals

An **improper fraction** has a numerator that is larger than its denominator. $\frac{19}{8}$ is an improper fraction.

$\frac{19}{8}$ means $19 \div 8$ or $8 \overline{\smash{)}19}$ with quotient 2, -16, remainder $3 \rightarrow 3 \div 8 = \frac{3}{8}$

This mixed numeral is written $2\frac{3}{8}$.

$\frac{19}{8} = 2\frac{3}{8}$

Change each improper fraction to a mixed numeral.

	a	b	c	d
1.	$\frac{23}{5}$ _____	$\frac{13}{4}$ _____	$\frac{15}{7}$ _____	$\frac{16}{9}$ _____
2.	$\frac{25}{6}$ _____	$\frac{5}{3}$ _____	$\frac{12}{5}$ _____	$\frac{15}{4}$ _____
3.	$\frac{17}{10}$ _____	$\frac{38}{7}$ _____	$\frac{14}{5}$ _____	$\frac{8}{3}$ _____
4.	$\frac{20}{3}$ _____	$\frac{7}{6}$ _____	$\frac{5}{2}$ _____	$\frac{4}{3}$ _____

Spectrum Fractions
Grade 6

Chapter 1
Understanding Fractions

Changing Mixed Numerals to Improper Fractions

To change a mixed numeral to a fraction, multiply the denominator by the whole number. Then, add the numerator to get the new numerator. Keep the denominator the same.

$4\frac{3}{5} = \frac{(5 \times 4) + 3}{5} = \frac{20 + 3}{5} = \frac{23}{5}$

$2\frac{3}{4} = \frac{(4 \times 2) + 3}{4} = \frac{8 + 3}{4} = \frac{11}{4}$

Change each mixed numeral to an improper fraction.

	a	b	c	d
1.	$2\frac{5}{8}$ _____	$3\frac{1}{4}$ _____	$2\frac{3}{7}$ _____	$4\frac{1}{2}$ _____
2.	$3\frac{3}{4}$ _____	$2\frac{5}{12}$ _____	$4\frac{1}{6}$ _____	$5\frac{2}{3}$ _____
3.	$2\frac{7}{16}$ _____	$3\frac{1}{2}$ _____	$1\frac{7}{16}$ _____	$2\frac{5}{8}$ _____
4.	$3\frac{1}{3}$ _____	$4\frac{2}{5}$ _____	$3\frac{1}{8}$ _____	$7\frac{1}{3}$ _____

Spectrum Fractions
Grade 6

Chapter 1
Understanding Fractions

Simplifying Mixed Numerals

SCORE ◯/16

A mixed numeral is in simplest form if its fraction is in simplest form and names a number less than 1.

The greatest common factor of 8 and 12 is 4.

$$3\frac{8}{12}$$
$$3 + \frac{8 \div 4}{12 \div 4} = \frac{2}{3}$$
$$3\frac{8}{12} = 3\frac{2}{3}$$

$$2\frac{9}{4} = 2 + \frac{9}{4}$$
$$2 + (2\frac{1}{4}) = 4\frac{1}{4}$$

↑ not in simplest form

Change each mixed numeral to simplest form.

	a	b	c	d
1.	$3\frac{6}{8}$ _____	$2\frac{12}{15}$ _____	$1\frac{9}{12}$ _____	$4\frac{10}{15}$ _____
2.	$2\frac{8}{5}$ _____	$3\frac{15}{4}$ _____	$1\frac{7}{3}$ _____	$2\frac{5}{2}$ _____
3.	$4\frac{4}{8}$ _____	$5\frac{6}{9}$ _____	$8\frac{12}{20}$ _____	$7\frac{4}{16}$ _____
4.	$2\frac{10}{4}$ _____	$3\frac{3}{2}$ _____	$7\frac{8}{12}$ _____	$5\frac{3}{9}$ _____

Spectrum Fractions
Grade 6

Chapter 1
Understanding Fractions

Check What You Learned

Understanding Fractions

Identify each number as prime (p) or composite (c).

a	b	c	d	e

1. 7 _____   21 _____   3 _____   27 _____   6 _____

Find the greatest common factor of the two numbers.

2. 16 and 24   21 and 14   9 and 45   13 and 25   12 and 45

   _____   _____   _____   _____   _____

Change each fraction to its simplest form.

3. $\frac{10}{25}$ _____ $\frac{21}{35}$ _____ $\frac{15}{24}$ _____ $\frac{16}{20}$ _____ $\frac{21}{24}$ _____

Rename each pair of fractions with common denominators.

4. $\frac{5}{8}$ and $\frac{7}{12}$ $\frac{3}{4}$ and $\frac{1}{6}$ $\frac{3}{5}$ and $\frac{2}{3}$ $\frac{3}{8}$ and $\frac{2}{3}$ $\frac{2}{7}$ and $\frac{5}{8}$

   _____   _____   _____   _____   _____

Spectrum Fractions
Grade 6

Check What You Learned

Understanding Fractions

Change each improper fraction to a mixed numeral.

a	b	c	d	e
5. $\frac{27}{8}$ _____	$\frac{18}{5}$ _____	$\frac{19}{6}$ _____	$\frac{35}{4}$ _____	$\frac{27}{5}$ _____

Change each mixed numeral to an improper fraction.

6. $4\frac{3}{7}$ _____ $2\frac{7}{16}$ _____ $3\frac{4}{5}$ _____ $7\frac{5}{6}$ _____ $6\frac{2}{3}$ _____

Change each mixed numeral to its simplest form.

7. $3\frac{7}{5}$ _____ $5\frac{12}{7}$ _____ $2\frac{8}{12}$ _____ $1\frac{11}{4}$ _____ $5\frac{5}{20}$ _____

NAME _____

 **Check What You Know**

Problem Solving: Understanding Fractions

Read the problem carefully and solve. Show your work under each question.

Lionel builds wooden furniture and sells them at his shop. This week, he plans to make 3 tables, 9 chairs, 15 stools, and 2 cabinets. After several days, he has completed $3\frac{7}{8}$ tables, $\frac{2}{3}$ of a chair, $13\frac{4}{14}$ stools, and $\frac{4}{5}$ of a cabinet.

1. Lionel looks at the numbers of each type of furniture he plans to make: 3, 9, 15, and 2. Which of these numbers are prime?

_____

2. Lionel compares the fractions that show how much of a chair and how much of a cabinet he has completed so far. Rename the pair of fractions so they have common denominators.

_____ and _____

3. How can the number of stools Lionel has completed be written as an improper fraction?

_____

4. Lionel wants to display the chairs and stools together in groups. Each display will have the same number of chairs and stools. What is the greatest common factor of 9 and 15?

_____

Spectrum Fractions
Grade 6

Chapter 2
Problem Solving: Understanding Fractions

17

Prime and Composite Numbers

Read the problem carefully and solve. Show your work under each question.

Lauren and her younger brother John compare their coins. They make the chart on the right, which shows the number of each type of coin they have.

	Lauren	John
Pennies	4	11
Nickels	13	9
Dimes	5	7
Quarters	8	15

> **Helpful Hint**
>
> A **prime number** is any number greater than 1 that has only two factors, itself and 1.
>
> A **composite number** has more than two factors.

1. Lauren looks at the numbers of coins on the chart. She notices that both of the numbers listed next to one type of coin are prime numbers. What is that coin?

   _____

2. Lauren also notices that one type of coin has only composite numbers listed on the chart. What is that coin?

   _____

3. Lauren has a total of 30 coins. Use a factor tree to find the prime factorization of 30.

   _____

NAME _____

SCORE ◯ /3

Reducing Fractions to Their Simplest Form

Read the problem carefully and solve. Show your work under each question.

Kamala owns a flower shop. Today, she arranges flowers into vases. She has 12 roses, 8 tulips, 18 lilies, and 10 daffodils. Kamala has 3 different colored vases: red, blue, and green.

1. Kamala arranges the roses and tulips together. She wants to put the same number of each flower in each vase, so she finds the greatest common factor of the number of roses and tulips. What is the greatest common factor of 12 and 8?

   _____

2. Kamala wants to arrange the lilies and daffodils together. She finds the greatest common factor of the number of lilies and daffodils. What is the greatest common factor of 18 and 10?

   _____

3. Kamala finds that $\frac{4}{18}$ of the lilies are wilted. What is this fraction written in its simplest form?

   _____

Spectrum Fractions
Grade 6

Chapter 2
Problem Solving: Understanding Fractions

Finding Common Denominators

SCORE ◯/5

Read the problem carefully and solve. Show your work under each question.

Mr. Blanco is the coach of the track team. As part of practice, he has several runners sprint around the track. After a few minutes, Mr. Blanco has the runners stop and record their distance. Their distances, in fractions of a mile, are on the chart at the right.

Andy	$\frac{2}{3}$ mile
Eartha	$\frac{7}{10}$ mile
Jerome	$\frac{3}{5}$ mile
Sarah	$\frac{7}{12}$ mile

Helpful Hint

The **least common multiple** of two numbers is the smallest number that is a multiple of both.

1. Mr. Blanco wants to compare Andy and Jerome's distances. Rename their fractions with a common denominator.

    _____ and _____

2. Mr. Blanco wants to compare Eartha and Jerome's distances. Rename their fractions with a common denominator.

    _____ and _____

3. Sarah says that she ran farther than Jerome. Rename their fractions with a common denominator and compare using >, <, or =.

    _____

Spectrum Fractions
Grade 6

Chapter 2
Problem Solving: Understanding Fractions

Changing Improper Fractions to Mixed Numerals

Read the problem carefully and solve. Show your work under each question.

Chelsea is baking muffins for the school bake sale. To make her famous blueberry bran muffins, Chelsea makes a list of the ingredients she needs. This list includes $\frac{40}{3}$ cups of flour, $\frac{42}{5}$ cups of milk, $\frac{8}{3}$ cups of brown sugar, $\frac{50}{7}$ cups of blueberries, and $\frac{7}{4}$ teaspoons of ground cinnamon.

---

1. Change the amount of ground cinnamon Chelsea needs to a mixed numeral.

_____ teaspoons

2. Change the amount of milk that Chelsea needs into a mixed numeral.

_____ cups

3. Chelsea buys a box of brown sugar that has $2\frac{1}{4}$ cups of brown sugar. Change the amount she needs for the recipe into a mixed numeral. Did she buy enough brown sugar?

_____ cups

_____

Spectrum Fractions
Grade 6

Chapter 2
Problem Solving: Understanding Fractions

21

NAME _____

SCORE ◯ /4

Changing Mixed Numerals to Improper Fractions

Read the problem carefully and solve. Show your work under each question.

Chelsea also makes granola bars for the bake sale, so she writes a list of the ingredients she needs. Some of the ingredients on this list are $2\frac{1}{2}$ sticks of butter, $4\frac{2}{7}$ cups of raisins, $1\frac{1}{5}$ cups of sesame seeds, $2\frac{2}{3}$ cups of brown sugar, $4\frac{1}{3}$ cups of almonds, and $14\frac{1}{4}$ cups of oats.

> **Helpful Hint**
> To change a mixed numeral into a fraction:
> 1. Multiply the denominator by the whole number.
> 2. Add the numerator.
> 3. Put this number over the original denominator.

1. Change the amount of sesame seeds Chelsea needs to an improper fraction.

_____ cups

2. Change the amount of raisins and almonds that Chelsea needs to improper fractions.

_____ cups of raisins

_____ cups of almonds

3. Does Chelsea need more raisins or almonds for her granola bar recipe? Explain your answer.

_____

Spectrum Fractions
Grade 6

Chapter 2
Problem Solving: Understanding Fractions

Simplifying Mixed Numerals

SCORE ◯ /3

Read the problem carefully and solve. Show your work under each question.

Benito volunteers at the local library. He made the chart on the right to show the number of hours he worked at the library each day last week.

Monday	$3\frac{8}{5}$ hours
Tuesday	$1\frac{15}{4}$ hours
Wednesday	$1\frac{7}{3}$ hours
Thursday	$1\frac{12}{8}$ hours
Friday	$3\frac{6}{8}$ hours

Helpful Hint

A mixed numeral is not in simplest form if:

1. The fraction is not reduced.
2. The fraction is improper.

1. Change the hours that Benito worked on Monday to a mixed numeral in its simplest form.

_____ hours

2. Change the hours that Benito worked on Tuesday to a mixed numeral in its simplest form.

_____ hours

3. Benito added up the hours he worked on Thursday and Friday. What is this number in its simplest form?

_____ hours

Spectrum Fractions
Grade 6

Chapter 2
Problem Solving: Understanding Fractions

23

NAME _____

SCORE ◯/7

Problem Solving

Solve each problem. Show your work under each question.

1. Show a factor tree and determine the prime factorization of 90.

_____

2. Find the greatest common factor of 28 and 32.

Factors of 28 are _____.

Factors of 32 are _____.

The greatest common factor is _____.

3. Find the least common multiple of 8 and 6.

Multiples of 8 are _____.

Multiples of 6 are _____.

The least common multiple is _____.

Spectrum Fractions
Grade 6

Chapter 2
Problem Solving: Understanding Fractions

24

Check What You Learned

Problem Solving: Understanding Fractions

Read the problem carefully and solve. Show your work under each question.

A group of teachers are helping Mr. Chen correct papers for his class. They have to correct 12 math tests, 9 book reports, 11 vocabulary quizzes, and 4 science tests. So far, they have corrected $5\frac{5}{6}$ math tests, $\frac{27}{5}$ book reports, $3\frac{19}{4}$ vocabulary quizzes, and $\frac{9}{12}$ of a science test.

1. Ms. Canales wants to compare the number of corrected book reports and the number of corrected science tests. What is the least common denominator for these fractions?

   _____

2. Ms. Jackson is correcting the science tests. How can $\frac{9}{12}$ be written in its simplest form?

   _____

3. Mr. Wood is correcting the vocabulary quizzes. How can the number of vocabulary quizzes that he has corrected so far be written as a mixed numeral in its simplest form?

   _____

4. Change the number of vocabulary quizzes corrected so far into an improper fraction in its simplest form.

   _____

Check What You Know

Adding and Subtracting Fractions

NAME _____

Add or subtract. Write answers in simplest form.

	a	b	c	d
1.	$\dfrac{3}{8}$ $+\dfrac{7}{8}$	$\dfrac{4}{5}$ $+\dfrac{3}{5}$	$\dfrac{2}{3}$ $+\dfrac{5}{8}$	$\dfrac{1}{3}$ $+\dfrac{1}{2}$
2.	$\dfrac{7}{8}$ $-\dfrac{5}{8}$	$\dfrac{11}{16}$ $-\dfrac{5}{16}$	$\dfrac{3}{4}$ $-\dfrac{1}{3}$	$\dfrac{5}{6}$ $-\dfrac{1}{2}$
3.	$2\dfrac{5}{8}$ $+1\dfrac{2}{3}$	$3\dfrac{1}{3}$ $+2\dfrac{3}{4}$	$5\dfrac{2}{5}$ $+2\dfrac{2}{3}$	$7\dfrac{2}{7}$ $+3\dfrac{1}{2}$
4.	$7\dfrac{2}{3}$ $-3\dfrac{1}{8}$	$6\dfrac{5}{6}$ $-2\dfrac{3}{4}$	$5\dfrac{1}{2}$ $-3\dfrac{2}{3}$	4 $-1\dfrac{3}{5}$
5.	$1\dfrac{3}{8}$ $2\dfrac{1}{3}$ $+\dfrac{5}{6}$	$2\dfrac{1}{8}$ $1\dfrac{1}{2}$ $+3\dfrac{1}{4}$	$3\dfrac{1}{2}$ $4\dfrac{1}{3}$ $+1\dfrac{3}{4}$	$2\dfrac{2}{5}$ $1\dfrac{1}{3}$ $+\dfrac{4}{5}$

CHAPTER 3 PRETEST

Spectrum Fractions
Grade 6

Chapter 3
Adding and Subtracting Fractions

26

Adding Fractions with Like Denominators

$$\begin{array}{r}\frac{7}{8}\\+\frac{3}{8}\\\hline\frac{10}{8}\end{array} = \frac{5}{4} = 1\frac{1}{4}$$

Add the numerators.

Use the same denominator.

Change to simplest form.

Add. Write answers in simplest form.

	a	b	c	d
1.	$\frac{3}{5} + \frac{4}{5}$	$\frac{1}{4} + \frac{3}{4}$	$\frac{2}{3} + \frac{2}{3}$	$\frac{5}{6} + \frac{3}{6}$
2.	$\frac{5}{7} + \frac{3}{7}$	$\frac{4}{9} + \frac{2}{9}$	$\frac{3}{4} + \frac{3}{4}$	$\frac{5}{6} + \frac{4}{6}$
3.	$\frac{1}{3} + \frac{1}{3}$	$\frac{5}{8} + \frac{7}{8}$	$\frac{5}{6} + \frac{2}{6}$	$\frac{8}{9} + \frac{5}{9}$
4.	$\frac{2}{5} + \frac{4}{5}$	$\frac{3}{4} + \frac{1}{4}$	$\frac{2}{7} + \frac{6}{7}$	$\frac{2}{5} + \frac{1}{5}$

NAME _____

Subtracting Fractions with Like Denominators

$$\begin{array}{r} \frac{5}{8} \\ -\frac{3}{8} \\ \hline \frac{2}{8} = \frac{1}{4} \end{array}$$

Subtract the numerators.

Use the same denominator.

Change to simplest form.

Subtract. Write answers in simplest form.

	a	b	c	d
1.	$\frac{5}{6} - \frac{1}{6}$	$\frac{7}{8} - \frac{1}{8}$	$\frac{3}{4} - \frac{1}{4}$	$\frac{5}{9} - \frac{1}{9}$
2.	$\frac{2}{3} - \frac{1}{3}$	$\frac{4}{6} - \frac{1}{6}$	$\frac{8}{9} - \frac{5}{9}$	$\frac{7}{8} - \frac{5}{8}$
3.	$\frac{9}{10} - \frac{7}{10}$	$\frac{4}{5} - \frac{2}{5}$	$\frac{5}{6} - \frac{2}{6}$	$\frac{7}{8} - \frac{4}{8}$
4.	$\frac{7}{12} - \frac{5}{12}$	$\frac{11}{12} - \frac{5}{12}$	$\frac{7}{12} - \frac{1}{12}$	$\frac{8}{9} - \frac{2}{9}$

Spectrum Fractions
Grade 6

Chapter 3
Adding and Subtracting Fractions

NAME _____

Adding and Subtracting with Unlike Denominators

Rename fractions with the lowest common denominator. Change to simplest form.

20 = least common multiple

$$\frac{4\,(\times 4)}{5\,(\times 4)} = \frac{16}{20}$$
$$+\frac{3\,(\times 5)}{4\,(\times 5)} = \frac{15}{20}$$
$$\frac{31}{20} = 1\frac{11}{20}$$

12 = least common multiple

$$\frac{3\,(\times 3)}{4\,(\times 3)} = \frac{9}{12}$$
$$-\frac{5}{12} = \frac{5}{12}$$
$$\frac{4}{12} = \frac{1}{3}$$

Add or subtract. Write answers in simplest form.

   a   **b**   **c**   **d**

1. $\frac{5}{8}$ $\frac{5}{6}$ $\frac{2}{3}$ $\frac{7}{10}$
   $+\frac{3}{4}$ $+\frac{3}{5}$ $+\frac{3}{4}$ $+\frac{1}{2}$

2. $\frac{3}{4}$ $\frac{7}{10}$ $\frac{7}{8}$ $\frac{3}{4}$
   $-\frac{5}{8}$ $-\frac{1}{2}$ $-\frac{1}{2}$ $-\frac{1}{3}$

3. $\frac{5}{12}$ $\frac{3}{8}$ $\frac{7}{9}$ $\frac{5}{8}$
   $+\frac{5}{6}$ $+\frac{3}{4}$ $+\frac{2}{3}$ $+\frac{1}{6}$

Spectrum Fractions
Grade 6

NAME _____

Adding and Subtracting with Unlike Denominators

Add or subtract. Write answers in simplest form.

	a	b	c	d
1.	$\frac{3}{4} + \frac{5}{8}$	$\frac{1}{2} + \frac{1}{3}$	$\frac{3}{4} + \frac{2}{5}$	$\frac{1}{6} + \frac{1}{3}$
2.	$\frac{3}{8} + \frac{4}{5}$	$\frac{1}{2} + \frac{3}{10}$	$\frac{2}{3} + \frac{3}{12}$	$\frac{3}{4} + \frac{7}{10}$
3.	$\frac{1}{4} + \frac{3}{8}$	$\frac{2}{5} + \frac{3}{7}$	$\frac{1}{7} + \frac{7}{8}$	$\frac{2}{3} + \frac{1}{5}$
4.	$\frac{3}{5} - \frac{1}{4}$	$\frac{1}{2} - \frac{3}{10}$	$\frac{7}{8} - \frac{1}{2}$	$\frac{4}{5} - \frac{1}{3}$
5.	$\frac{3}{4} - \frac{2}{3}$	$\frac{5}{9} - \frac{1}{2}$	$\frac{1}{2} - \frac{1}{3}$	$\frac{7}{11} - \frac{2}{9}$

Spectrum Fractions
Grade 6

Chapter 3
Adding and Subtracting Fractions

Adding Mixed Numerals with Unlike Denominators

$2\frac{1}{2}\frac{(\times 4)}{(\times 4)}$ $2\frac{4}{8}$ Rename fractions with common denominators. $3\frac{3}{4}\frac{(\times 2)}{(\times 2)}$ $3\frac{6}{8}$
$+3\frac{3}{8}$ $+3\frac{3}{8}$ Add the fractions. Add the whole numbers. $+2\frac{5}{8}$ $+2\frac{5}{8}$
                    $5\frac{7}{8}$ Simplify. $5\frac{11}{8}$
                                                                                                $5 + 1\frac{3}{8} = 6\frac{3}{8}$

Add. Write answers in simplest form.

    a   **b**   **c**   **d**

1. $3\frac{2}{5}$ $7\frac{3}{8}$ $4\frac{1}{2}$ $5\frac{1}{2}$
     $+2\frac{3}{10}$ $+\frac{3}{4}$ $+2\frac{2}{3}$ $+\frac{5}{6}$

2. $2\frac{3}{4}$ $2\frac{1}{2}$ $3\frac{2}{3}$ $1\frac{1}{8}$
     $+1\frac{1}{6}$ $+3\frac{5}{8}$ $+\frac{5}{6}$ $+3\frac{3}{4}$

3. $1\frac{1}{2}$ $2\frac{3}{8}$ $\frac{2}{3}$ $2\frac{3}{8}$
     $2\frac{1}{3}$ $3\frac{1}{4}$ $1\frac{1}{2}$ $3\frac{1}{2}$
    $+\frac{3}{4}$ $+2\frac{1}{2}$ $+2\frac{1}{4}$ $+1\frac{1}{4}$

NAME _____

Subtracting Mixed Numerals with Unlike Denominators

$$5\tfrac{3}{4} \tfrac{(\times 3)=}{(\times 3)=} \quad 5\tfrac{9}{12}$$
$$-2\tfrac{2}{3} \tfrac{(\times 4)=}{(\times 4)=} \quad -2\tfrac{8}{12}$$
$$\overline{\phantom{-2\tfrac{2}{3}} \quad 3\tfrac{1}{12}}$$

Rename.

$$4\tfrac{1}{3} = 3 + 1\tfrac{1}{3} = 3\tfrac{4}{3}$$
$$-1\tfrac{2}{3} \phantom{= 3 + 1\tfrac{1}{3} =} -1\tfrac{2}{3}$$
$$\overline{\phantom{-1\tfrac{2}{3} = 3 + 1\tfrac{1}{3} =} \quad 2\tfrac{2}{3}}$$

Subtract. Write answers in simplest form.

	a	b	c	d
1.	4 $-\tfrac{3}{8}$	$5\tfrac{5}{6}$ $-1\tfrac{1}{3}$	8 $-3\tfrac{5}{8}$	$4\tfrac{3}{5}$ $-\tfrac{3}{10}$
2.	$5\tfrac{3}{4}$ $-4\tfrac{5}{8}$	$8\tfrac{2}{3}$ $-4\tfrac{1}{6}$	$5\tfrac{5}{6}$ $-3\tfrac{3}{4}$	$7\tfrac{4}{5}$ $-2\tfrac{1}{2}$
3.	$5\tfrac{3}{8}$ $-2\tfrac{7}{8}$	$3\tfrac{1}{4}$ $-2\tfrac{3}{4}$	$8\tfrac{2}{5}$ $-3\tfrac{4}{5}$	$1\tfrac{1}{3}$ $-\tfrac{2}{3}$
4.	$4\tfrac{3}{4}$ $-2\tfrac{7}{8}$	$6\tfrac{1}{2}$ $-3\tfrac{2}{3}$	5 $-2\tfrac{3}{5}$	3 $-\tfrac{5}{6}$

Spectrum Fractions
Grade 6

Chapter 3
Adding and Subtracting Fractions

NAME _____

Adding and Subtracting Mixed Numerals

Add or subtract. Write answers in simplest form.

	a	b	c	d
1.	$1\frac{1}{3}$ $+2\frac{1}{4}$	$3\frac{3}{8}$ $+7\frac{1}{2}$	$4\frac{2}{7}$ $+2\frac{1}{3}$	$1\frac{2}{5}$ $+3\frac{3}{10}$
2.	$4\frac{4}{9}$ $+3\frac{1}{3}$	$1\frac{1}{8}$ $+1\frac{7}{10}$	$2\frac{1}{6}$ $+3\frac{5}{8}$	$1\frac{3}{7}$ $+2\frac{1}{5}$
3.	$3\frac{1}{2}$ $+2\frac{1}{4}$	$2\frac{5}{6}$ $+1\frac{5}{9}$	$3\frac{4}{7}$ $+1\frac{1}{10}$	$4\frac{1}{3}$ $+2\frac{1}{2}$
4.	$2\frac{3}{8}$ $-1\frac{2}{9}$	$3\frac{1}{4}$ $-1\frac{1}{3}$	$4\frac{1}{2}$ $-3\frac{3}{4}$	$6\frac{5}{8}$ $-4\frac{6}{7}$
5.	$3\frac{2}{11}$ $-1\frac{5}{8}$	$7\frac{2}{3}$ $-3\frac{2}{5}$	$5\frac{1}{3}$ $-2\frac{1}{2}$	$2\frac{5}{6}$ $-1\frac{2}{7}$
6.	$4\frac{7}{9}$ $-2\frac{2}{3}$	$3\frac{1}{5}$ $-1\frac{3}{4}$	$4\frac{5}{6}$ $-2\frac{1}{8}$	$3\frac{1}{8}$ $-1\frac{3}{4}$

Spectrum Fractions
Grade 6

Chapter 3
Adding and Subtracting Fractions

NAME _____

Check What You Learned

Adding and Subtracting Fractions

Add or subtract. Write answers in simplest form.

	a	b	c	d
1.	$\frac{4}{3} + \frac{4}{3}$	$\frac{3}{8} + \frac{2}{3}$	$\frac{1}{3} + \frac{1}{4}$	$\frac{2}{5} + \frac{3}{4}$
2.	$\frac{9}{16} - \frac{3}{16}$	$\frac{5}{6} - \frac{5}{8}$	$\frac{3}{4} - \frac{3}{5}$	$\frac{7}{8} - \frac{2}{5}$
3.	$2\frac{3}{8} + 3\frac{1}{3}$	$1\frac{1}{4} + 2\frac{5}{6}$	$5\frac{3}{8} + 3\frac{1}{2}$	$4\frac{4}{7} + 3\frac{2}{3}$
4.	$6\frac{3}{4} - 2\frac{2}{3}$	$2\frac{5}{7} - 1\frac{2}{3}$	$4\frac{1}{2} - 1\frac{5}{6}$	$7 - 3\frac{4}{7}$
5.	$3\frac{5}{8} + 1\frac{2}{3} + \frac{1}{6}$	$2\frac{5}{6} + 3\frac{1}{2} + 2\frac{1}{3}$	$5\frac{1}{2} + 4\frac{1}{6} + 2\frac{3}{4}$	$1\frac{3}{6} + 1\frac{1}{3} + 2\frac{4}{5}$

Spectrum Fractions
Grade 6

Check What You Know

Problem Solving: Adding and Subtracting Fractions

Read the problem carefully and solve. Show your work under each question.

Members of the soccer team meet every day at the park for practice. The chart below shows how far six members of the soccer team live from the park.

Ayame	Cindy	Della	Lita	Mandy	Susan
$\frac{7}{8}$ mile	$2\frac{2}{3}$ miles	$4\frac{2}{5}$ miles	$\frac{3}{8}$ mile	$5\frac{3}{7}$ miles	$\frac{3}{5}$ mile

1. Ayame and Lita both walk from their homes to the park. How much farther does Ayame walk?

   _____ mile

2. After practice, Lita and Ayame go to Lita's house together. What total distance does Ayame walk from her house to the park and from the park to Lita's house?

   _____ miles

3. How much farther does Susan live from the park than Lita?

   _____ mile

4. Cindy and Della both ride their bicycles to practice. What is the combined distance from their houses to the park?

   _____ miles

Spectrum Fractions
Grade 6

Adding Like Fractions

Read the problem carefully and solve. Show your work under each question.

Marc wraps presents at the shopping center for charity. He uses spools of red, green, blue, and purple ribbon. For each present that he wraps, Marc measures the ribbon in fractions of a meter.

1. Marc wraps a book using $\frac{3}{5}$ meter of red ribbon and $\frac{1}{5}$ meter of purple ribbon. How much total ribbon does Marc use to wrap the book?

   _____ meter

2. Marc wraps a toy using $\frac{8}{9}$ meter of green ribbon and $\frac{5}{9}$ meter of blue ribbon. How much total ribbon does Marc use to wrap the toy?

   _____ meters

3. Marc wraps a stereo using 2 green ribbons. The green ribbons are $\frac{2}{7}$ meter and $\frac{6}{7}$ meter long. What is the total length of the green ribbons that Marc uses to wrap the stereo?

   _____ meters

NAME _____

SCORE ⬜/3

Adding and Subtracting with Unlike Denominators

Read the problem carefully and solve. Show your work under each question.

Rosa and Tom are in charge of the food for their grandmother's birthday party. They set out 2 pitchers of juice, 2 blocks of cheese, a box of crackers, and a large bowl of salad.

Helpful Hint

Rename fractions with the least common denominator and change to simplest form.

Example: $\frac{2}{3} + \frac{1}{2}$

$\frac{4}{6} + \frac{3}{6} = \frac{7}{6} = 1\frac{1}{6}$

---

1. Tom is serving juice. He serves $\frac{5}{8}$ of a pitcher. An hour later, he serves $\frac{3}{4}$ of the other pitcher. How much juice has he served in all?

   _____ pitchers

2. Rosa checks to see how much of the cheese has been eaten. One block has $\frac{2}{3}$ left, and the other has $\frac{3}{4}$ left. How much cheese is left?

   _____ blocks

3. After one hour, the box of crackers has $\frac{5}{6}$ left. Later, $\frac{1}{3}$ of the box of crackers is left. What is the difference between these fractions?

   _____

Spectrum Fractions
Grade 6

Chapter 4
Problem Solving: Adding and Subtracting Fractions

Adding Mixed Numerals with Unlike Denominators

SCORE /2

Read the problem carefully and solve. Show your work under each question.

A group of sixth graders participate in a charity walkathon. People from the area have pledged money to the students. The farther they walk, the more money they raise. After an hour, Dylan has walked $2\frac{5}{6}$ miles, Meredith has walked $1\frac{5}{9}$ miles, Aida has walked $2\frac{1}{3}$ miles, Taci has walked $3\frac{1}{5}$ miles, and Ellis has walked $3\frac{1}{2}$ miles.

> **Helpful Hint**
> When adding three mixed numerals, rename the fractions so that all three have one common denominator. Remember to simplify the answer.

1. Mr. and Mrs. Gonzales have pledged money to Dylan, Meredith, and Ellis. How far have these three students walked?

    _____ miles

2. Ms. Gomez says that she will pledge money to the 3 students in the group who walk the farthest. What is the combined distance of these students?

    _____ miles

Spectrum Fractions
Grade 6

Chapter 4
Problem Solving: Adding and Subtracting Fractions

NAME _____

SCORE ◯ /3

Adding Mixed Numerals with Unlike Denominators

3. Ms. Hyoshi pledged money to both Aida and Dylan. How far altogether have Aida and Dylan walked?

_____ miles

4. Mr. Franklin has pledged money to Aida and Ellis. How far have they walked in all?

_____ miles

5. Mr. Agoyo, Taci's father, wants to know how far she and her friend Meredith have walked. What is this total?

_____ miles

Spectrum Fractions
Grade 6

Chapter 4
Problem Solving: Adding and Subtracting Fractions

NAME _____

Subtracting Mixed Numerals with Unlike Denominators

Read the problem carefully and solve. Show your work under each question.

After the charity walkathon, Dylan made the chart on the right. The chart shows the total distance each student walked. Dylan wants to use the chart to compare everyone's distances.

Aida	$8\frac{3}{4}$
Dylan	$7\frac{1}{2}$
Ellis	$9\frac{3}{5}$
Meredith	$6\frac{7}{12}$
Taci	$4\frac{1}{6}$

Helpful Hint

Rename if necessary. Simplify your answer.

$$4\frac{1}{4} \longrightarrow 3\frac{5}{4}$$
$$-1\frac{3}{4} \longrightarrow -1\frac{3}{4}$$
$$\overline{2\frac{2}{4} = 2\frac{1}{2}}$$

1. How much farther did Dylan walk than Meredith?

_____ mile

2. The three girls walked for a total of 7 hours. The two boys walked for a total of $4\frac{5}{6}$ hours. What is the difference?

_____ hours

Spectrum Fractions
Grade 6
40

NAME _____

Subtracting Mixed Numerals with Unlike Denominators

3. How much farther did Aida walk than Dylan?

_____ miles

4. How much farther did Dylan walk than Taci?

_____ miles

5. How much farther did Ellis walk than Meredith?

_____ miles

Check What You Learned

Problem Solving: Adding and Subtracting Fractions

Read the problem carefully and solve. Show your work under each question.

Francisco made a chart of the number of hours he studied each day this week.

Monday	Tuesday	Wednesday	Thursday	Friday
$\frac{2}{7}$ hour	$\frac{6}{7}$ hour	$3\frac{1}{6}$ hours	$2\frac{3}{4}$ hours	$1\frac{2}{3}$ hours

1. How long did Francisco study on Monday and Tuesday in total?

_____ hours

2. On Tuesday, Francisco studied math and science only. He studied math for $\frac{1}{2}$ hour. How long did he study science?

_____ hour

3. How long did Francisco study on Thursday and Friday in total?

_____ hours

4. On Wednesday, Francisco studied social studies and spelling only. He studied social studies for $1\frac{4}{5}$ hours. How long did he study spelling?

_____ hours

Spectrum Fractions
Grade 6

Chapter 4
Problem Solving: Adding and Subtracting Fractions

Mid-Test Chapters 1–4

Write the prime factorization of each number.

	a	b	c
1.	40	54	36

Find the least common multiple for each pair of numbers.

2.	6 and 10	9 and 15	8 and 7

Add. Write answers in simplest form.

	a	b	c	d
3.	$\frac{3}{8} + \frac{2}{3}$	$\frac{2}{3} + \frac{7}{10}$	$2\frac{1}{6} + 3\frac{2}{3}$	$1\frac{1}{2} + \frac{2}{3}$
4.	$\frac{5}{6} + 2\frac{1}{3}$	$3\frac{1}{4} + 2\frac{1}{2}$	$3\frac{5}{8} + 2\frac{1}{4} + 2\frac{1}{2}$	$3\frac{1}{2} + 2\frac{1}{3} + \frac{1}{12}$

Subtract. Write answers in simplest form.

	a	b	c	d
5.	$\frac{5}{9} - \frac{1}{3}$	$\frac{5}{6} - \frac{1}{4}$	$\frac{9}{10} - \frac{2}{5}$	$\frac{3}{4} - \frac{2}{3}$
6.	$3\frac{1}{4} - 2\frac{3}{4}$	$8\frac{2}{3} - 4\frac{1}{6}$	$1\frac{1}{3} - \frac{2}{3}$	$8 - 3\frac{5}{8}$

Spectrum Fractions
Grade 6

Mid-Test Chapters 1–4

Solve each problem. Show your work under each question.

7. In a recent year, it rained 8 out of the 28 days in February. Write a fraction (in simplest form) showing the days in February that it rained.

It rained _____ days.

8. Of 128 members of the school chorus, 96 are sopranos. What fraction (in simplest form) of the members of the school chorus are sopranos?

_____ of the members of the school chorus are sopranos.

9. Maria babysat her brothers for $1\frac{2}{3}$ hours on Monday and $2\frac{1}{2}$ hours on Wednesday. How many total hours did she babysit on those two days? How much longer did she babysit on Wednesday than on Monday?

She babysat for _____ hours.

She babysat _____ of an hour more on Wednesday.

10. On Monday, Paula bought $12\frac{1}{8}$ gallons of gas for her car. On Friday, she bought another $6\frac{3}{5}$ gallons. How many gallons did she buy on these two days?

Paula bought _____ gallons of gas.

Check What You Know

Multiplying and Dividing Fractions

Multiply or divide. Write answers in simplest form.

	a	b	c
1.	$\frac{7}{8} \times \frac{3}{4}$	$9 \times \frac{3}{8}$	$\frac{5}{8} \times 5$
2.	$3\frac{1}{8} \times 4$	$8 \times 2\frac{3}{5}$	$4\frac{1}{2} \times 9$
3.	$5\frac{3}{4} \times 2\frac{1}{3}$	$2\frac{1}{4} \times 3\frac{1}{5}$	$3\frac{2}{3} \times 1\frac{1}{8}$
4.	$8 \div \frac{2}{3}$	$\frac{4}{5} \div 3$	$10 \div \frac{3}{8}$
5.	$\frac{4}{5} \div \frac{7}{8}$	$\frac{2}{3} \div \frac{5}{6}$	$\frac{3}{8} \div \frac{7}{8}$
6.	$2\frac{3}{4} \div 3\frac{1}{8}$	$7 \div 3\frac{1}{4}$	$7\frac{3}{8} \div 9$

Spectrum Fractions
Grade 6

Chapter 5
Multiplying and Dividing Fractions

45

NAME _____

Multiplying Fractions

Multiply fractions.

$\frac{3}{8} \times \frac{2}{3} = \frac{3 \times 2}{8 \times 3}$ Multiply numerators together. Multiply denominators together.

$= \frac{6}{24} = \frac{1}{4}$ Simplify.

Multiply. Write answers in simplest form.

	a	b	c
1.	$\frac{2}{5} \times \frac{2}{3}$	$\frac{3}{4} \times \frac{5}{6}$	$\frac{7}{8} \times \frac{5}{7}$
2.	$\frac{7}{12} \times \frac{3}{4}$	$\frac{2}{3} \times \frac{8}{9}$	$\frac{4}{5} \times \frac{3}{8}$
3.	$\frac{1}{6} \times \frac{2}{3}$	$\frac{11}{12} \times \frac{2}{3}$	$\frac{2}{5} \times \frac{2}{5}$
4.	$\frac{2}{9} \times \frac{3}{8}$	$\frac{5}{8} \times \frac{1}{6}$	$\frac{8}{9} \times \frac{2}{3}$

Spectrum Fractions
Grade 6

Chapter 5
Multiplying and Dividing Fractions

NAME _____

Multiplying Fractions

Multiply. Write answers in simplest form.

	a	b	c	d
1.	$\frac{1}{2} \times \frac{3}{4}$	$\frac{2}{3} \times \frac{4}{5}$	$\frac{3}{4} \times \frac{3}{4}$	$\frac{4}{5} \times \frac{1}{8}$
2.	$\frac{3}{5} \times \frac{7}{8}$	$\frac{1}{3} \times \frac{3}{5}$	$\frac{3}{7} \times \frac{1}{5}$	$\frac{3}{10} \times \frac{4}{5}$
3.	$\frac{5}{8} \times \frac{3}{8}$	$\frac{2}{3} \times \frac{1}{2}$	$\frac{5}{6} \times \frac{2}{3}$	$\frac{4}{7} \times \frac{1}{3}$
4.	$\frac{1}{2} \times \frac{1}{3}$	$\frac{2}{3} \times \frac{3}{5}$	$\frac{2}{3} \times \frac{1}{5}$	$\frac{1}{3} \times \frac{5}{8}$
5.	$\frac{1}{4} \times \frac{3}{4}$	$\frac{1}{3} \times \frac{3}{4}$	$\frac{3}{7} \times \frac{2}{3}$	$\frac{5}{8} \times \frac{2}{3}$
6.	$\frac{3}{7} \times \frac{1}{2}$	$\frac{4}{9} \times \frac{3}{5}$	$\frac{7}{8} \times \frac{2}{5}$	$\frac{4}{5} \times \frac{3}{4}$

Spectrum Fractions
Grade 6

Chapter 5
Multiplying and Dividing Fractions

NAME _____

Multiplying Fractions and Whole Numbers

$\frac{3}{5} \times 8$
$\frac{3}{5} \times \frac{8}{1} = \frac{24}{5}$ Rename 8 as $\frac{8}{1}$.
$\phantom{\frac{3}{5} \times \frac{8}{1}} = 4\frac{4}{5}$ Write in simplest form.

$5 \times \frac{2}{3}$
$\frac{5}{1} \times \frac{2}{3} = \frac{10}{3}$ Rename 5 as $\frac{5}{1}$.
$\phantom{\frac{5}{1} \times \frac{2}{3}} = 3\frac{1}{3}$ Write in simplest form.

Multiply. Write answers in simplest form.

	a	b	c	d
1.	$3 \times \frac{5}{8}$	$8 \times \frac{4}{5}$	$6 \times \frac{2}{3}$	$4 \times \frac{7}{8}$
2.	$\frac{3}{5} \times 6$	$\frac{5}{12} \times 9$	$\frac{3}{7} \times 4$	$\frac{5}{8} \times 6$
3.	$10 \times \frac{2}{5}$	$5 \times \frac{5}{8}$	$3 \times \frac{4}{7}$	$2 \times \frac{3}{4}$
4.	$\frac{3}{10} \times 8$	$\frac{2}{3} \times 7$	$\frac{3}{4} \times 9$	$\frac{1}{2} \times 5$

Spectrum Fractions
Grade 6

Chapter 5
Multiplying and Dividing Fractions

NAME _____

Multiplying Mixed Numbers and Whole Numbers

$2\frac{3}{4} \times 5$
$\frac{11}{4} \times \frac{5}{1}$
$= \frac{55}{4} = 13\frac{3}{4}$

Rename the mixed number and the whole number as improper fractions.
Multiply.
Write in simplest form.

Multiply. Write answers in simplest form.

	a	b	c	d
1.	$1\frac{1}{2} \times 5$	$2\frac{1}{4} \times 3$	$8 \times 3\frac{1}{2}$	$4 \times 3\frac{1}{2}$
2.	$7 \times 3\frac{3}{8}$	$6 \times 2\frac{3}{4}$	$2\frac{1}{3} \times 4$	$3\frac{1}{8} \times 5$
3.	$1\frac{1}{4} \times 6$	$3\frac{1}{2} \times 7$	$5 \times 2\frac{1}{8}$	$4 \times 2\frac{1}{4}$
4.	$2 \times 2\frac{3}{7}$	$8 \times 4\frac{3}{5}$	$2\frac{1}{3} \times 3$	$5\frac{3}{8} \times 2$

Spectrum Fractions
Grade 6

Chapter 5
Multiplying and Dividing Fractions

NAME _____

Multiplying Mixed Numbers

$2\frac{3}{4} \times 3\frac{1}{3}$
$\frac{11}{4} \times \frac{10}{3} = \frac{110}{12} = \frac{55}{6}$
$\quad\quad = 9\frac{1}{6}$

Rename each mixed numeral as an improper fraction.
Multiply.
Simplify.

Multiply. Write answers in simplest form.

	a	b	c	d
1.	$1\frac{1}{3} \times 2\frac{1}{8}$	$2\frac{1}{2} \times 1\frac{3}{4}$	$2\frac{5}{8} \times 2\frac{3}{5}$	$1\frac{1}{2} \times 2\frac{2}{3}$
2.	$3\frac{1}{5} \times 5\frac{2}{3}$	$4\frac{1}{2} \times 4\frac{1}{2}$	$2\frac{1}{3} \times 3\frac{1}{4}$	$2\frac{4}{5} \times 3\frac{1}{8}$
3.	$2\frac{2}{3} \times 5\frac{1}{4}$	$2\frac{1}{3} \times 2\frac{1}{3}$	$3\frac{1}{4} \times 1\frac{1}{8}$	$2\frac{7}{8} \times 1\frac{1}{3}$
4.	$2\frac{5}{8} \times 2\frac{1}{4}$	$1\frac{1}{8} \times 1\frac{3}{5}$	$1\frac{1}{6} \times 2\frac{3}{8}$	$4\frac{1}{2} \times 3\frac{1}{3}$

Spectrum Fractions
Grade 6

Chapter 5
Multiplying and Dividing Fractions

NAME _____

SCORE / 18

Multiplying Mixed Numbers

Multiply. Write answers in simplest form.

	a	b	c
1.	$3 \times 1\frac{2}{7}$	$2\frac{1}{4} \times 3\frac{1}{3}$	$1\frac{1}{9} \times 3\frac{1}{4}$
2.	$2\frac{1}{4} \times 6$	$1\frac{2}{3} \times 3\frac{7}{8}$	$2\frac{1}{7} \times 1\frac{1}{3}$
3.	$4\frac{1}{2} \times 2\frac{1}{3}$	$5\frac{1}{4} \times 2\frac{1}{2}$	$4\frac{1}{8} \times 3\frac{2}{7}$
4.	$\frac{5}{6} \times 1\frac{1}{3}$	$\frac{2}{3} \times 1\frac{5}{8}$	$1\frac{1}{2} \times 2\frac{2}{3}$
5.	$2\frac{1}{4} \times 1\frac{1}{8}$	$\frac{5}{6} \times 1\frac{3}{8}$	$2\frac{1}{4} \times 1\frac{1}{3}$
6.	$5 \times 1\frac{1}{7}$	$1\frac{1}{7} \times \frac{5}{8}$	$1\frac{1}{9} \times \frac{3}{8}$

Spectrum Fractions
Grade 6

Chapter 5
Multiplying and Dividing Fractions

NAME _____

Multiplication Practice

Multiply. Write answers in simplest form.

	a	b	c	d
1.	$\frac{2}{3} \times \frac{4}{5}$	$\frac{3}{8} \times \frac{5}{8}$	$\frac{2}{7} \times \frac{4}{5}$	$\frac{2}{3} \times \frac{3}{8}$
2.	$\frac{1}{2} \times \frac{3}{7}$	$\frac{3}{4} \times \frac{3}{4}$	$5 \times \frac{2}{3}$	$4 \times \frac{2}{3}$
3.	$2 \times \frac{7}{16}$	$\frac{3}{8} \times 4$	$\frac{2}{5} \times 6$	$\frac{3}{4} \times 5$
4.	$2\frac{3}{4} \times 3$	$2\frac{7}{8} \times 6$	$3\frac{1}{3} \times 8$	$5 \times 2\frac{4}{5}$
5.	$3 \times 4\frac{5}{8}$	$5 \times 3\frac{2}{3}$	$2\frac{1}{5} \times 1\frac{1}{8}$	$1\frac{4}{7} \times 2\frac{3}{5}$
6.	$3\frac{1}{2} \times 3\frac{1}{3}$	$2\frac{2}{7} \times 2\frac{1}{8}$	$2\frac{1}{2} \times 4\frac{1}{4}$	$2\frac{3}{8} \times 1\frac{1}{2}$

Spectrum Fractions
Grade 6

Chapter 5
Multiplying and Dividing Fractions

Reciprocals

The product of a number and its reciprocal is 1.

$\frac{3}{5}$ and $\frac{5}{3}$ are reciprocals.

$\frac{3}{5} \times \frac{5}{3} = \frac{15}{15} = 1$

The reciprocal of $\frac{3}{5}$ is $\frac{5}{3}$.

Find the reciprocal of a whole number by writing it as a fraction.

$4 = \frac{4}{1}$

The reciprocal of 4 is $\frac{1}{4}$.

Write the reciprocal.

	a	b	c	d	e	f
1.	$\frac{2}{3}$	$\frac{5}{8}$	$\frac{1}{4}$	$\frac{3}{8}$	$\frac{1}{6}$	$\frac{3}{7}$
2.	2	3	5	9	8	5
3.	7	$\frac{7}{3}$	$\frac{1}{3}$	$\frac{1}{2}$	$\frac{3}{4}$	$\frac{1}{5}$
4.	$\frac{4}{5}$	$\frac{5}{6}$	$\frac{1}{7}$	$\frac{11}{8}$	$\frac{6}{7}$	$\frac{10}{3}$
5.	$\frac{1}{9}$	$\frac{11}{4}$	$\frac{5}{9}$	$\frac{4}{9}$	$\frac{5}{2}$	6
6.	$\frac{7}{10}$	$\frac{2}{5}$	1	$\frac{1}{15}$	$\frac{7}{9}$	$\frac{7}{16}$

NAME _____

Dividing Whole Numbers and Fractions

To divide, multiply by the reciprocal of the divisor.

$$6 \div \tfrac{3}{8} = 6 \times \tfrac{8}{3}$$
$$= \tfrac{6}{1} \times \tfrac{8}{3}$$
$$= \tfrac{48}{3} = 16$$

$$\tfrac{4}{5} \div 8 = \tfrac{4}{5} \times \tfrac{1}{8}$$
$$= \tfrac{4}{40}$$
$$= \tfrac{1}{10}$$

Divide. Write answers in simplest form.

	a	b	c	d
1.	$5 \div \tfrac{2}{3}$	$6 \div \tfrac{5}{8}$	$2 \div \tfrac{4}{5}$	$8 \div \tfrac{3}{7}$
2.	$9 \div \tfrac{3}{4}$	$10 \div \tfrac{5}{6}$	$15 \div \tfrac{3}{5}$	$4 \div \tfrac{7}{8}$
3.	$\tfrac{7}{8} \div 5$	$\tfrac{5}{8} \div 6$	$\tfrac{9}{10} \div 4$	$\tfrac{4}{5} \div 12$
4.	$\tfrac{4}{7} \div 7$	$\tfrac{5}{6} \div 8$	$\tfrac{5}{12} \div 5$	$\tfrac{2}{3} \div 4$

Spectrum Fractions
Grade 6

NAME _____

Dividing Fractions by Fractions

To divide, multiply by the reciprocal of the divisor.

$$\frac{4}{5} \div \frac{8}{9} = \frac{4}{5} \times \frac{9}{8} = \frac{36}{40} = \frac{9}{10}$$

Divide. Write answers in simplest form.

	a	b	c	d
1.	$\frac{1}{2} \div \frac{3}{5}$	$\frac{3}{8} \div \frac{2}{3}$	$\frac{5}{8} \div \frac{3}{4}$	$\frac{2}{5} \div \frac{3}{8}$
2.	$\frac{1}{2} \div \frac{7}{8}$	$\frac{4}{5} \div \frac{3}{4}$	$\frac{5}{6} \div \frac{3}{8}$	$\frac{2}{3} \div \frac{4}{5}$
3.	$\frac{7}{8} \div \frac{1}{3}$	$\frac{7}{9} \div \frac{2}{3}$	$\frac{1}{3} \div \frac{2}{3}$	$\frac{5}{6} \div \frac{1}{3}$
4.	$\frac{3}{5} \div \frac{2}{3}$	$\frac{4}{9} \div \frac{3}{7}$	$\frac{1}{2} \div \frac{5}{8}$	$\frac{2}{3} \div \frac{7}{9}$

NAME _____

Dividing Mixed Numbers

$3\frac{2}{5} \div 4$ Rename $3\frac{2}{5}$ as $\frac{17}{5}$. $4\frac{1}{3} \div 2\frac{3}{4}$

$\frac{17}{5} \div \frac{4}{1}$ Rename 4 as $\frac{4}{1}$. $\frac{13}{3} \div \frac{11}{4}$ Rename.

$\frac{17}{5} \times \frac{1}{4} = \frac{17}{20}$ Multiply by the reciprocal. $\frac{13}{3} \times \frac{4}{11} = \frac{52}{33} = 1\frac{19}{33}$ Multiply by the reciprocal.

Divide. Write answers in simplest form.

	a	**b**	**c**	**d**
1.	$2\frac{1}{2} \div 3\frac{1}{3}$	$1\frac{1}{8} \div 2\frac{1}{4}$	$8 \div 3\frac{1}{2}$	$2\frac{2}{3} \div 5$
2.	$4\frac{1}{2} \div 1\frac{1}{6}$	$4\frac{5}{6} \div 2\frac{2}{5}$	$4\frac{1}{3} \div 6$	$1\frac{1}{2} \div 3\frac{1}{8}$
3.	$6 \div 2\frac{1}{2}$	$1\frac{1}{2} \div 3$	$5 \div 3\frac{3}{4}$	$2\frac{1}{8} \div 3$
4.	$3\frac{3}{5} \div 4$	$3\frac{1}{3} \div 2\frac{3}{8}$	$1 \div 4\frac{1}{3}$	$9 \div 1\frac{2}{3}$

NAME _____

Dividing Fractions and Mixed Numerals

Divide. Write answers in simplest form.

	a	b	c	d
1.	$3\frac{1}{2} \div \frac{2}{3}$	$4\frac{3}{4} \div 1\frac{7}{8}$	$\frac{3}{4} \div \frac{1}{2}$	$2\frac{2}{3} \div \frac{1}{8}$
2.	$7 \div \frac{3}{5}$	$2\frac{1}{12} \div 1\frac{1}{3}$	$2\frac{1}{7} \div \frac{3}{4}$	$3 \div \frac{1}{5}$
3.	$1\frac{1}{8} \div \frac{1}{10}$	$1\frac{2}{5} \div 2\frac{1}{3}$	$5 \div 1\frac{1}{2}$	$3\frac{1}{4} \div 1\frac{1}{2}$
4.	$6\frac{2}{3} \div \frac{2}{3}$	$3\frac{1}{8} \div \frac{2}{7}$	$4\frac{1}{4} \div \frac{1}{12}$	$14 \div \frac{1}{7}$
5.	$2\frac{3}{5} \div 1\frac{2}{7}$	$1\frac{1}{9} \div \frac{7}{11}$	$2 \div \frac{3}{4}$	$2\frac{4}{5} \div 3$

Spectrum Fractions
Grade 6

Chapter 5
Multiplying and Dividing Fractions

Division Practice

Write the reciprocals.

a	b	c	d
1. $\frac{3}{4}$ _____	$\frac{11}{8}$ _____	3 _____	$\frac{2}{5}$ _____

Divide. Write answers in simplest form.

a	b	c	d
2. $2 \div \frac{3}{8}$	$4 \div \frac{2}{5}$	$6 \div \frac{4}{7}$	$3 \div \frac{7}{8}$
3. $\frac{3}{4} \div \frac{1}{2}$	$\frac{4}{5} \div \frac{2}{3}$	$\frac{3}{8} \div \frac{7}{12}$	$\frac{4}{5} \div \frac{5}{6}$
4. $5 \div 3\frac{1}{2}$	$2 \div 4\frac{1}{3}$	$6 \div 2\frac{2}{3}$	$7 \div 3\frac{1}{2}$
5. $5\frac{2}{3} \div 4$	$3\frac{1}{8} \div 5$	$4\frac{3}{5} \div 6$	$1\frac{7}{8} \div 3$
6. $3\frac{1}{2} \div 5\frac{2}{3}$	$4\frac{1}{3} \div 3\frac{1}{2}$	$2\frac{2}{3} \div 1\frac{3}{4}$	$1\frac{7}{8} \div 2\frac{1}{2}$

Spectrum Fractions
Grade 6

NAME _____

Multiplication and Division Practice

Multiply or divide. Write answers in simplest form.

	a	b	c	d
1.	$\frac{1}{3} \times \frac{3}{8}$	$\frac{7}{6} \times \frac{4}{13}$	$\frac{3}{7} \times \frac{4}{5}$	$\frac{2}{3} \times \frac{1}{2}$
2.	$\frac{1}{2} \times \frac{5}{12}$	$\frac{2}{3} \times \frac{5}{9}$	$\frac{1}{8} \times \frac{2}{7}$	$\frac{3}{5} \times \frac{2}{3}$
3.	$\frac{1}{2} \times 1\frac{2}{5}$	$\frac{5}{7} \times 2\frac{1}{8}$	$1\frac{1}{2} \times 2\frac{1}{4}$	$3\frac{1}{8} \times 4\frac{1}{4}$
4.	$3\frac{1}{3} \times \frac{1}{4}$	$1\frac{5}{8} \times 2\frac{1}{3}$	$3\frac{4}{7} \times 1\frac{4}{5}$	$3\frac{1}{4} \times 2\frac{1}{8}$
5.	$\frac{3}{5} \div \frac{2}{7}$	$\frac{3}{4} \div \frac{1}{2}$	$\frac{5}{8} \div \frac{3}{5}$	$\frac{5}{6} \div \frac{1}{10}$
6.	$5 \div 1\frac{1}{4}$	$3\frac{1}{2} \div \frac{2}{3}$	$1\frac{6}{7} \div 2\frac{1}{8}$	$3\frac{1}{4} \div 2$

Spectrum Fractions
Grade 6

Check What You Learned

Multiplying and Dividing Fractions

Multiply or divide. Write answers in simplest form.

	a	b	c	d
1.	$\frac{2}{3} \times \frac{3}{4}$	$\frac{1}{2} \times \frac{3}{8}$	$\frac{7}{8} \times \frac{3}{5}$	$\frac{2}{7} \times \frac{5}{8}$
2.	$\frac{2}{3} \times 5$	$4 \times \frac{7}{8}$	$\frac{3}{5} \times 12$	$8 \times \frac{4}{7}$
3.	$3\frac{1}{8} \times 4$	$5 \times 7\frac{1}{2}$	$3\frac{2}{3} \times 6$	$10 \times 1\frac{2}{3}$
4.	$2\frac{1}{2} \times 3\frac{1}{3}$	$1\frac{1}{5} \times 3\frac{3}{4}$	$2\frac{1}{2} \times 2\frac{1}{2}$	$4\frac{1}{3} \times 2\frac{3}{5}$
5.	$5 \div \frac{2}{3}$	$\frac{4}{5} \div 5$	$7 \div \frac{3}{8}$	$\frac{7}{8} \div 2$
6.	$\frac{2}{3} \div \frac{4}{5}$	$\frac{7}{8} \div \frac{2}{3}$	$\frac{4}{7} \div \frac{3}{8}$	$\frac{5}{12} \div \frac{3}{4}$
7.	$3\frac{1}{8} \div 2\frac{1}{2}$	$4\frac{2}{3} \div 3\frac{1}{2}$	$2\frac{3}{4} \div 2\frac{3}{4}$	$1\frac{1}{2} \div 3\frac{1}{8}$

CHAPTER 5 POSTTEST

Spectrum Fractions
Grade 6

Chapter 5
Multiplying and Dividing Fractions

Check What You Know

Problem Solving: Multiplying and Dividing Fractions

Read the problem carefully and solve. Show your work under each question.

Ms. Vega's class is planning a party to thank all the parents who helped their class during the year. The class spends time preparing for the party. The students want to make gifts for the parents. Many of them bring in supplies from home to make their gifts.

1. Before lunch, Mario and Sean together painted $\frac{6}{8}$ of a banner thanking the parents. Sean painted $\frac{2}{3}$ of that amount. What part of the banner did Sean paint?

   _____ of the banner

2. Cara brought in $\frac{6}{9}$ yard of blue ribbon to make her gift. She cuts the ribbon into 3 equal pieces. What is the length of each piece?

   _____ yard

3. Inez brought in $\frac{7}{8}$ yard of red ribbon. She cuts the ribbon into pieces that are each $\frac{1}{5}$ yard long. How many pieces did she cut?

   _____ pieces

4. Ms. Vega's class spends $\frac{3}{4}$ hour preparing for the party each day. How many hours do they spend in 4 days?

   _____ hours

Multiplying Fractions

SCORE /3

Read the problem carefully and solve. Show your work under each question.

Keiko and her brother Masako volunteer to rake yards for some of the people in their neighborhood. Every day, they take turns raking different amounts of each neighbor's yard.

1. Keiko and Masako together raked $\frac{2}{5}$ of Mrs. Franklin's yard before they had to go to dinner. Keiko raked $\frac{3}{4}$ of that amount. What part of the yard did Keiko rake?

   _____ of the yard

2. Before soccer practice, Keiko and Masako together raked $\frac{3}{4}$ of Mr. Garcia's yard. Masako raked $\frac{1}{3}$ of that amount. What part of the yard did Masako rake?

   _____ of the yard

3. Keiko and Masako bagged $\frac{5}{8}$ of the pile of leaves they raked from Mr. Wong's yard before dark. Keiko bagged $\frac{2}{3}$ of that amount. What portion of the leaves did Keiko bag?

   _____ of the leaves

Spectrum Fractions
Grade 6

Chapter 6
Problem Solving: Multiplying and Dividing Fractions

Multiplying Mixed Numbers

SCORE /3

Read the problem carefully and solve. Show your work under each question.

Gary's Garden Shop sells bags of grass seed, sand, and potting soil. The potting soil comes in small and large sizes. The grass seed and sand come in three different sizes: small, medium, and large.

> **Helpful Hint**
>
> Remember to rename each mixed numeral as an improper fraction before multiplying.
>
> Be sure to simplify all fractions.

1. The small bag of potting soil weighs $3\frac{1}{4}$ pounds. The large bag weighs $3\frac{2}{3}$ times more than the small bag. How much does the large bag weigh?

   _____ pounds

2. The medium bag of sand weighs $2\frac{1}{4}$ times more than the small bag. The small bag of sand weighs $5\frac{1}{2}$ pounds. How much does the medium bag weigh?

   _____ pounds

3. The large bag of sand weighs $3\frac{3}{4}$ times more than the small bag. How much does the large bag of sand weigh?

   _____ pounds

Spectrum Fractions
Grade 6

Chapter 6
Problem Solving: Multiplying and Dividing Fractions

NAME _____

SCORE ◯ /3

Multiplying Fractions and Mixed Numbers by Whole Numbers

Read the problem carefully and solve. Show your work under each question.

Emily does a lot of activities during the week. Emily spends $\frac{3}{4}$ of an hour practicing piano every day. She also has basketball practice for $1\frac{2}{5}$ hours and spends $\frac{2}{3}$ of an hour walking her dog each day.

1. How many hours does Emily spend at basketball practice in 5 days?

   _____ hours

2. Emily likes to walk her dog before she goes to school. How many hours does she walk her dog in 5 days?

   _____ hours

3. After basketball season is over, Emily plans to take an art class after school for 4 days each week. The class lasts for $1\frac{1}{4}$ hours each time. How many total hours will she have art class each week?

   _____ hours

Spectrum Fractions
Grade 6

Dividing Fractions by Fractions

Read the problem carefully and solve. Show your work under each question.

Jonah is helping his grandfather cut 4 pieces of wood. His grandfather plans to cut each piece of wood into equal parts. The first piece of wood is $\frac{3}{4}$ meter long. The second piece of wood is $\frac{4}{5}$ meter long. The third piece is $\frac{2}{3}$ meter long, and the fourth piece is $\frac{7}{8}$ meter long.

> **Helpful Hint**
>
> To divide two fractions, multiply the first fraction by the reciprocal of the second fraction.
>
> $\frac{3}{4} \div \frac{5}{9} = \frac{3}{4} \times \frac{9}{5}$
>
> Simplify all fractions.

1. Jonah's grandfather cuts the first piece of wood into pieces that are $\frac{1}{3}$ meter long. How many pieces can be cut?

_____ pieces

2. Jonah wants to cut the second piece of wood into pieces that are $\frac{2}{3}$ meter long. How many pieces will he have?

_____ pieces

3. Jonah's grandfather decides to cut the third piece of wood into pieces that are $\frac{1}{2}$ meter long. How many pieces will he have?

_____ pieces

Dividing Whole Numbers and Fractions

SCORE ◯ /3

Read the problem carefully and solve. Show your work under each question.

Kenesha and Leon need to use colored ribbons for a craft project. They plan to cut each color ribbon into equal parts. The blue ribbon is $\frac{2}{3}$ yard long, and the yellow ribbon is $\frac{3}{4}$ yard long. The white ribbon is $\frac{6}{8}$ yard long, and the red ribbon is $\frac{3}{5}$ yard long.

1. What is the reciprocal of the amount of blue ribbon Kenesha and Leon have?

   _____

2. Kenesha cut the blue ribbon into 4 pieces. What is the length of each piece?

   _____ yard

3. Leon decides to cut the yellow ribbon into 6 pieces. What is the length of each piece?

   _____ yard

Spectrum Fractions
Grade 6

NAME _____

SCORE ⬤ /3

Dividing Mixed Numbers

Read the problem carefully and solve. Show your work under each question.

Emilio is having guests over for a cookout. He divides the food equally into bowls and containers to spread around for his guests.

1. Emilio has $6\frac{1}{4}$ ounces of nuts. He plans to divide the nuts into containers that hold $2\frac{1}{2}$ ounces each. How many containers will he fill?

   _____ containers

2. Emilio made $3\frac{3}{4}$ pounds of fruit salad. He plans to divide it evenly into containers that hold $1\frac{2}{5}$ pounds each. How many containers will he fill?

   _____ containers

3. Before Emilio divides up the fruit salad, he decides he wants to put it into 3 bowls instead. How many pounds of fruit salad will be in each bowl?

   _____ pounds

Spectrum Fractions
Grade 6

Chapter 6
Problem Solving: Multiplying and Dividing Fractions

Check What You Learned

Problem Solving: Multiplying and Dividing Fractions

Read the problem carefully and solve. Show your work under each question.

Adita and Amit want to make a garden. They look for supplies around their house. They find $\frac{3}{5}$ yard of ribbon and a piece of wood $\frac{4}{5}$ meter long. Their mother buys them a $4\frac{3}{4}$-pound bag of fertilizer.

1. Adita and Amit together dug up the soil in $\frac{2}{3}$ of the garden before lunch. Amit dug $\frac{1}{4}$ of that amount. What part of the garden did Amit dig?

   _____ of the garden

2. Their dad helps them cut the piece of wood into stakes for the tomato plants. He cuts the wood into pieces that are $\frac{1}{3}$ meter long. How many pieces does he cut?

   _____ pieces

3. Adita plans to tie each of the tomato plants to a stake. She cuts the piece of ribbon into 6 equal pieces. What is the length of each piece?

   _____ yard

4. Adita and Amit spend $1\frac{2}{3}$ hours working on the garden every day. How many hours do they spend working on it in 5 days?

   _____ hours

Spectrum Fractions
Grade 6

Check What You Know

Fractions and Decimals

Change the fractions to decimals.

	a	b	c	d	e
1.	$\frac{2}{10}$ _____	$\frac{23}{100}$ _____	$\frac{2}{5}$ _____	$\frac{3}{4}$ _____	$\frac{49}{50}$ _____

Change the decimals to fractions or mixed numerals in simplest form.

2. 0.6 _____   0.08 _____   2.25 _____   3.15 _____   2.2 _____

Convert each fraction to a decimal.

	a	b	c
	Convert to tenths.	Convert to hundredths.	Convert to thousandths.
3.	$1\frac{3}{5}$ _____	$2\frac{1}{4}$ _____	$\frac{48}{200}$ _____
4.	$2\frac{1}{2}$ _____	$5\frac{6}{25}$ _____	$2\frac{23}{500}$ _____
5.	$5\frac{4}{5}$ _____	$1\frac{7}{20}$ _____	$6\frac{157}{250}$ _____
6.	$6\frac{1}{5}$ _____	$2\frac{9}{10}$ _____	$3\frac{72}{100}$ _____

Spectrum Fractions
Grade 6

Chapter 7
Fractions and Decimals

NAME _____

SCORE ◯ / 22

Tenths and Hundredths

Numbers like 0.2, 3.4, 0.05, and 2.16 are called **decimals**.

$\frac{2}{10} = 0.2$ or two tenths $\frac{5}{100} = 0.05$ or five hundredths

↕ decimal point

$3\frac{4}{10} = 3.4$ or three and four tenths $2\frac{16}{100} = 2.16$ or two and sixteen hundredths

Write each fraction or mixed numeral as a decimal.

	a	b	c	d
1.	$\frac{3}{10}$ _____	$\frac{1}{10}$ _____	$\frac{7}{100}$ _____	$\frac{4}{100}$ _____
2.	$2\frac{4}{10}$ _____	$7\frac{6}{10}$ _____	$21\frac{2}{100}$ _____	$58\frac{9}{100}$ _____

Write each decimal as a fraction or mixed numeral.

| 3. | 0.4 _____ | 0.8 _____ | 0.06 _____ | 0.39 _____ |
| 4. | 9.6 _____ | 13.3 _____ | 11.16 _____ | 689.05 _____ |

Write a decimal for each of the following.

	a	b
5.	nine tenths _____	eight hundredths _____
6.	five and two tenths _____	three and two hundredths _____
7.	one tenth _____	seventy-three hundredths _____

Spectrum Fractions
Grade 6

Chapter 7
Fractions and Decimals

NAME _____

Thousandths and Ten Thousandths

$\frac{3}{1000}$ = 0.003 or three thousandths

$4\frac{23}{1000}$ = 4.023 or four and twenty-three thousandths

$\frac{5}{10000}$ = 0.0005 or five ten thousandths

$2\frac{53}{10000}$ = 2.0053 or two and fifty-three ten thousandths

---

Write each fraction or mixed numeral as a decimal.

	a	b	c
1.	$\frac{7}{1000}$ _____	$\frac{25}{1000}$ _____	$\frac{561}{1000}$ _____
2.	$\frac{4}{10000}$ _____	$\frac{435}{10000}$ _____	$\frac{508}{10000}$ _____
3.	$2\frac{5}{1000}$ _____	$7\frac{861}{1000}$ _____	$4\frac{128}{1000}$ _____
4.	$5\frac{31}{10000}$ _____	$2\frac{165}{10000}$ _____	$8\frac{8}{10000}$ _____

Write each decimal as a fraction or mixed numeral.

5.	0.002 _____	0.089 _____	0.082 _____
6.	0.733 _____	0.4125 _____	0.0315 _____
7.	3.0201 _____	6.223 _____	4.301 _____
8.	25.1367 _____	3.1416 _____	7.2003 _____

Spectrum Fractions
Grade 6

Chapter 7
Fractions and Decimals

Changing Fractions to Decimals

Change $\frac{1}{5}$ to tenths.

$\frac{1}{5} = \frac{1 \times 2}{5 \times 2} = \frac{2}{10} = 0.2$

Change $\frac{1}{4}$ to hundredths.

$\frac{1}{4} = \frac{1 \times 25}{4 \times 25} = \frac{25}{100} = 0.25$

Change $\frac{1}{5}$ to hundredths.

$\frac{1}{5} = \frac{1 \times 20}{5 \times 20} = \frac{20}{100} = 0.20$

Change $\frac{1}{250}$ to thousandths.

$3\frac{1}{250} = 3\frac{1 \times 4}{250 \times 4} = 3\frac{4}{1000} = 3.004$

Change each of the following to a decimal as indicated.

	a	b	c
1.	Change $\frac{2}{5}$ to tenths.	Change $\frac{2}{5}$ to hundredths.	Change $\frac{2}{5}$ to thousandths.
2.	Change $3\frac{1}{2}$ to tenths.	Change $\frac{3}{25}$ to hundredths.	Change $\frac{17}{25}$ to thousandths.
3.	Change $2\frac{3}{5}$ to tenths.	Change $\frac{9}{20}$ to hundredths.	Change $\frac{29}{250}$ to thousandths.

Spectrum Fractions
Grade 6

Changing Fractions to Decimals

Change each of the following to a decimal as indicated.

	a	b	c
1.	Change $2\frac{1}{5}$ to tenths.	Change $\frac{17}{50}$ to hundredths.	Change $1\frac{27}{100}$ to thousandths.
2.	Change $\frac{4}{5}$ to tenths.	Change $\frac{3}{4}$ to hundredths.	Change $\frac{3}{40}$ to thousandths.
3.	Change $7\frac{1}{2}$ to tenths.	Change $2\frac{3}{10}$ to hundredths.	Change $\frac{7}{125}$ to thousandths.
4.	Change $1\frac{3}{5}$ to tenths.	Change $\frac{3}{20}$ to hundredths.	Change $3\frac{72}{100}$ to thousandths.
5.	Change $6\frac{1}{5}$ to tenths.	Change $5\frac{6}{25}$ to hundredths.	Change $2\frac{23}{500}$ to thousandths.
6.	Change $\frac{2}{5}$ to tenths.	Change $2\frac{1}{4}$ to hundredths.	Change $\frac{12}{25}$ to thousandths.

Spectrum Fractions
Grade 6

Chapter 7
Fractions and Decimals

NAME _____

SCORE

Changing Decimals to Fractions

$0.4 = \frac{4}{10} = \frac{2}{5}$

$0.19 = \frac{19}{100}$

$2.35 = 2\frac{35}{100} = 2\frac{7}{20}$

$0.125 = \frac{125}{1000} = \frac{1}{8}$

$3.24 = 3\frac{24}{100} = 3\frac{6}{25}$

Write each decimal as a fraction or mixed numeral in simplest form.

	a	b	c	d
1.	0.4 _____	0.75 _____	3.1 _____	0.6 _____
2.	0.25 _____	1.3 _____	4.15 _____	2.2 _____
3.	3.127 _____	0.16 _____	8.4 _____	2.5 _____
4.	0.001 _____	0.04 _____	1.6 _____	1.01 _____

Spectrum Fractions
Grade 6

Chapter 7
Fractions and Decimals

NAME _____

Changing Decimals to Fractions

Write each decimal as a fraction or mixed numeral in simplest form.

     a   **b**   **c**   **d**

1. 0.64 _____   0.70 _____   4.6 _____   0.88 _____

2. 2.42 _____   0.56 _____   0.15 _____   0.002 _____

3. 2.3 _____   3.9 _____   1.95 _____   0.442 _____

4. 1.86 _____   3.31 _____   0.96 _____   0.12 _____

5. 4.76 _____   3.89 _____   4.08 _____   0.55 _____

Spectrum Fractions
Grade 6

Chapter 7
Fractions and Decimals

Check What You Learned

Fractions and Decimals

Change the fractions to decimals.

	a	b	c	d	e
1.	$\frac{4}{10}$ _____	$\frac{37}{1000}$ _____	$\frac{1}{5}$ _____	$\frac{1}{4}$ _____	$\frac{23}{50}$ _____

Change the decimals to fractions or mixed numerals in simplest form.

2. 0.16 _____   0.95 _____   2.75 _____   3.5 _____   4.01 _____

Convert each decimal to a fraction or mixed numeral in simplest form.

	a	b	c
3.	0.3 _____	1.6 _____	3.7 _____
4.	0.75 _____	5.86 _____	1.13 _____
5.	0.387 _____	2.588 _____	3.090 _____
6.	0.5329 _____	6.4273 _____	5.5825 _____

Spectrum Fractions
Grade 6

Final Test Chapters 1–7

Label each number as prime or composite.

	a	b	c
1.	17 _____	21 _____	77 _____
2.	82 _____	51 _____	25 _____

Find the greatest common factor for each set of numbers.

3. 18 and 22 _____   25 and 50 _____   54 and 36 _____

4. 40 and 8 _____   16, 24, and 18 _____   32, 8, and 40 _____

Write out the prime factorization for each number.

5. 6 _____   21 _____   12 _____

6. 25 _____   32 _____   44 _____

Reduce each fraction to simplest form.

7. $\frac{6}{9}$ _____ $\frac{12}{36}$ _____ $\frac{20}{32}$ _____

8. $\frac{21}{49}$ _____ $\frac{15}{18}$ _____ $\frac{40}{45}$ _____

9. $\frac{12}{14}$ _____ $\frac{19}{38}$ _____ $\frac{27}{30}$ _____

Spectrum Fractions
Grade 6

Final Test
Chapters 1–7

Final Test: Chapters 1–7

Add, subtract, multiply, or divide. Write answers in simplest form.

	a	b	c	d
10.	$\frac{3}{8} + 1\frac{5}{7}$	$2\frac{1}{4} + 3\frac{1}{3}$	$1\frac{5}{6} + 2\frac{7}{8}$	$4\frac{3}{4} + 2\frac{3}{8}$
11.	$4\frac{2}{3} - 1\frac{1}{4}$	$\frac{7}{8} - \frac{1}{2}$	$4\frac{3}{10} - 1\frac{6}{7}$	$5\frac{1}{4} - 2\frac{5}{6}$
12.	$\frac{3}{8} \times \frac{4}{5}$	$\frac{1}{2} \times \frac{3}{7}$	$\frac{5}{9} \times \frac{1}{3}$	$\frac{2}{3} \times \frac{1}{4}$
13.	$3\frac{2}{7} \times \frac{5}{8}$	$2\frac{3}{4} \times 1\frac{2}{7}$	$3\frac{2}{3} \times 1\frac{5}{6}$	$2\frac{1}{3} \times 1\frac{1}{2}$
14.	$6\frac{1}{8} \div 2\frac{4}{7}$	$3\frac{2}{3} \div 8$	$5\frac{1}{2} \div 1\frac{2}{5}$	$\frac{3}{4} \div \frac{1}{8}$

Spectrum Fractions
Grade 6

Final Test: Chapters 1–7

Add, subtract, multiply, or divide. Write answers in simplest form.

	a	b	c	d	e
15.	$\frac{5}{6} + \frac{1}{6}$	$\frac{3}{4} + \frac{2}{3}$	$\frac{3}{8} + \frac{5}{6}$	$4\frac{2}{3} + 3\frac{1}{4}$	$2\frac{1}{6} + 2\frac{1}{3}$
16.	$\frac{7}{8} - \frac{5}{8}$	$\frac{5}{6} - \frac{2}{3}$	$6 - \frac{3}{5}$	$5\frac{3}{4} - 2\frac{2}{3}$	$6\frac{1}{2} - 3\frac{5}{6}$
17.	$5 \times \frac{1}{6}$	$\frac{3}{5} \div 4$	$\frac{7}{8} \div \frac{2}{3}$	$4\frac{1}{3} \times 5$	$3\frac{1}{8} \div 1\frac{2}{3}$

Change each of the following to a decimal as indicated.

	a	b	c
18.	$2\frac{1}{2}$ to tenths	$2\frac{1}{2}$ to hundredths	$2\frac{1}{2}$ to thousandths

Change each decimal to a fraction or mixed numeral in simplest form.

19. 0.38 _____   0.08 _____   0.012 _____

20. 2.14 _____   3.9 _____   154.083 _____

Spectrum Fractions
Grade 6

Final Test Chapters 1–7

NAME _____

Solve each problem. Write answers in simplest form.

21. Alice and Samantha watered $\frac{5}{6}$ of the yard together. Samantha watered $\frac{1}{3}$ of that amount. What part of the yard did Samantha water?

Samantha watered _____ of the yard.

22. Ramona sets aside $\frac{3}{4}$ hour for homework after school each day. How many hours does she do homework in 5 days?

Ramona does _____ hours of homework in 5 days.

23. Miki is making bows. She needs $5\frac{3}{4}$ inches of ribbon for one and $3\frac{2}{3}$ inches for the other. How much ribbon does she need for both bows?

She needs _____ inches.

24. Carla has a length of ribbon that is 14 inches long. How much will be left if she uses $10\frac{1}{4}$ inches of it?

_____ inches of ribbon will be left.

Spectrum Fractions
Grade 6
80

Final Test Chapters 1–7

Solve each problem. Show your work.

25. John and George together raked $\frac{7}{8}$ of the yard. John raked $\frac{3}{4}$ of that amount. What part of the yard did John rake?

John raked _____ of the yard.

26. Felipe has track practice for $\frac{5}{8}$ of an hour after school each day. How many hours does he have track practice in 5 days?

Felipe has track practice for _____ hours.

27. Paul can walk $2\frac{1}{2}$ miles in 1 hour. How far can he walk in $1\frac{3}{4}$ hours?

Paul can walk _____ miles.

28. Brad has a stack of 7 books on his desk. Each book is $1\frac{7}{8}$ inches thick. How tall is the stack?

The stack is _____ inches tall.

Final Test Chapters 1–7

NAME _____

Solve each problem. Show your work.

29. A stack of 5 bricks is on the driveway. Each brick is $2\frac{1}{3}$ inches thick. How high is the stack of bricks?

The stack of bricks is _____ inches high.

30. At the grocery, the bags of oranges weigh $4\frac{1}{3}$ pounds. How much would $2\frac{1}{2}$ bags of oranges weigh?

The $2\frac{1}{2}$ bags would weigh _____ pounds.

31. It takes a baseball team 2 hours to complete a game. How long will it take to complete $\frac{2}{3}$ of the game?

It will take _____ hours.

32. A bag holding $7\frac{1}{5}$ pounds of mixed nuts will be divided equally among 9 people. How many pounds of nuts will each person get?

Each person will get _____ of a pound of nuts.

Spectrum Fractions
Grade 6

Scoring Record for Pretests, Posttests, Mid-Test, and Final Test

NAME _____

Pretests, Posttests, Mid-Test, and Final Test	Your Score	Performance			
		Excellent	Very Good	Fair	Needs Improvement
Chapter 1 Pretest	___ of 35	34–35	29–33	22–28	21 or fewer
Chapter 1 Posttest	___ of 35	34–35	29–33	22–28	21 or fewer
Chapter 2 Pretest	___ of 5	5	4	3	2 or fewer
Chapter 2 Posttest	___ of 4	4	3	2	1
Chapter 3 Pretest	___ of 20	19–20	16–18	13–15	12 or fewer
Chapter 3 Posttest	___ of 20	19–20	16–18	13–15	12 or fewer
Chapter 4 Pretest	___ of 4	4	3	2	1
Chapter 4 Posttest	___ of 4	4	3	2	1
Chapter 5 Pretest	___ of 18	17–18	15–16	11–14	10 or fewer
Chapter 5 Posttest	___ of 28	26–28	23–26	18–22	17 or fewer
Chapter 6 Pretest	___ of 4	4	3	2	1
Chapter 6 Posttest	___ of 4	4	3	2	1
Chapter 7 Pretest	___ of 22	21–22	18–20	14–17	13 or fewer
Chapter 7 Posttest	___ of 22	21–22	18–20	14–17	13 or fewer
Mid-Test	___ of 27	26–27	22–25	17–21	16 or fewer
Final Test	___ of 83	79–83	68–78	50–67	49 or fewer

Spectrum Fractions
Grade 6

Scoring Record

Answer Key

Answer Key

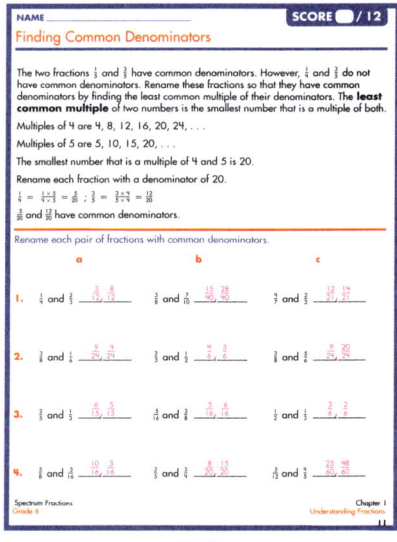

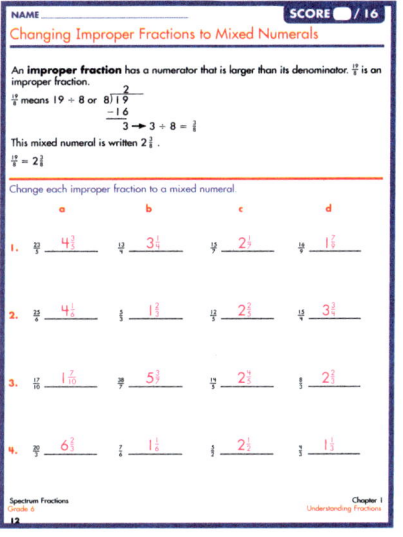

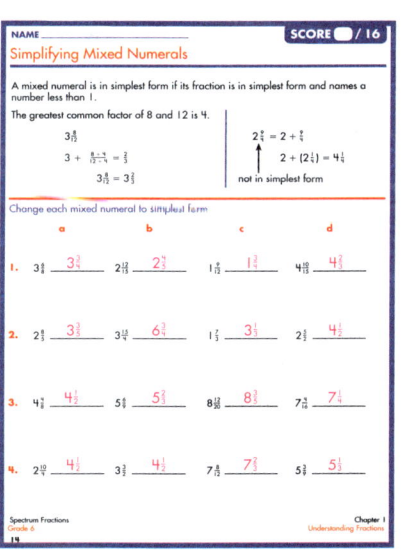

Answer Key

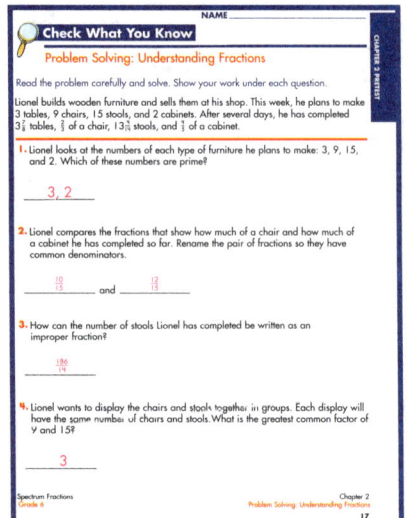
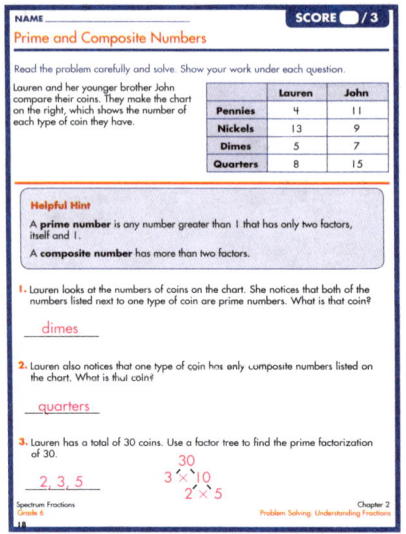

Answer Key

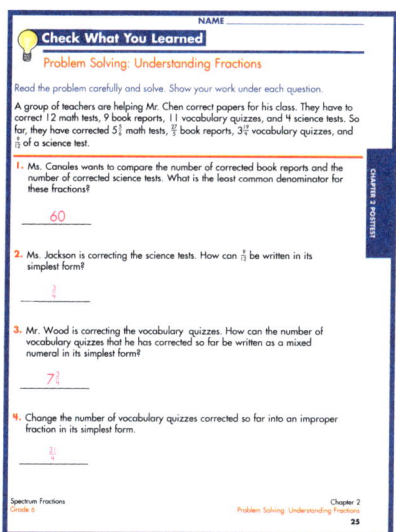

Answer Key

Spectrum Fractions
Grade 6

Answer Key

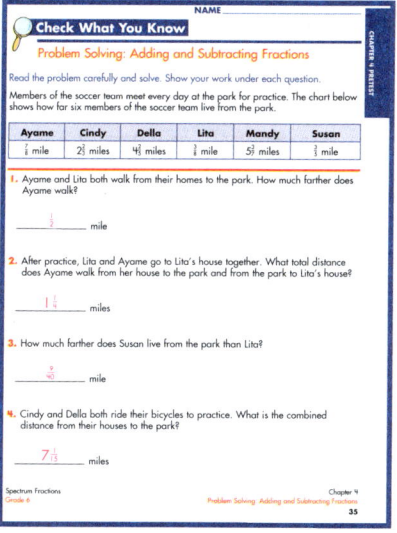

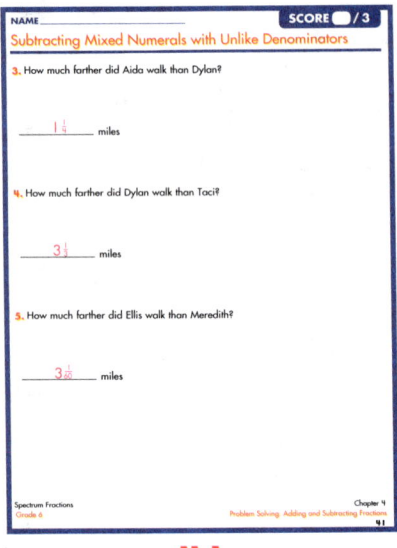

Answer Key

Answer Key

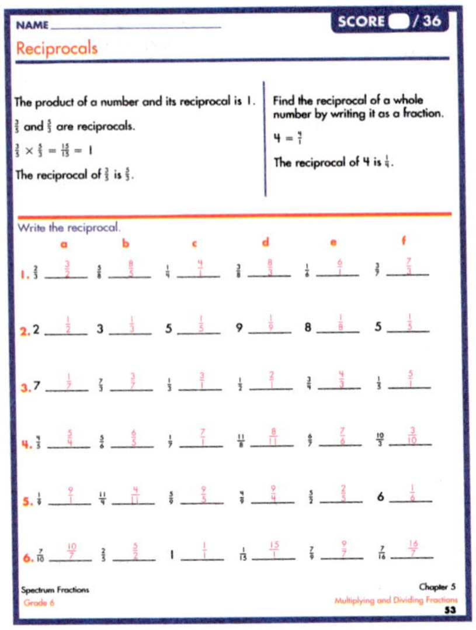

NAME

SCORE / 36

Reciprocals

The product of a number and its reciprocal is 1.

Find the reciprocal of a whole number by writing it as a fraction.

Write the reciprocal.

Spectrum Fractions
Grade 6

Chapter 5
Multiplying and Dividing Fractions
53

53

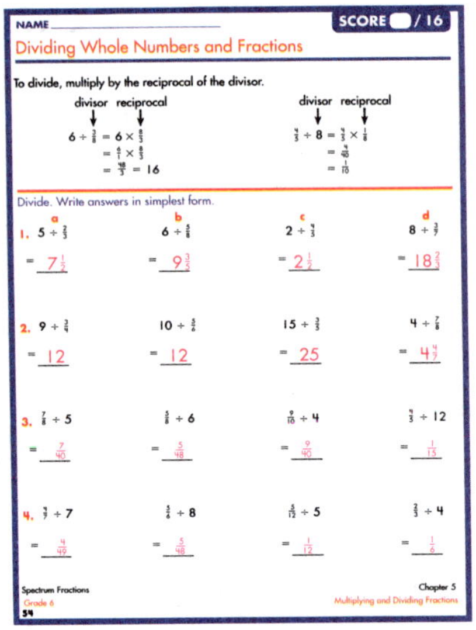

NAME

SCORE / 16

Dividing Whole Numbers and Fractions

To divide, multiply by the reciprocal of the divisor.

Divide. Write answers in simplest form.

Spectrum Fractions
Grade 6
54

Chapter 5
Multiplying and Dividing Fractions

54

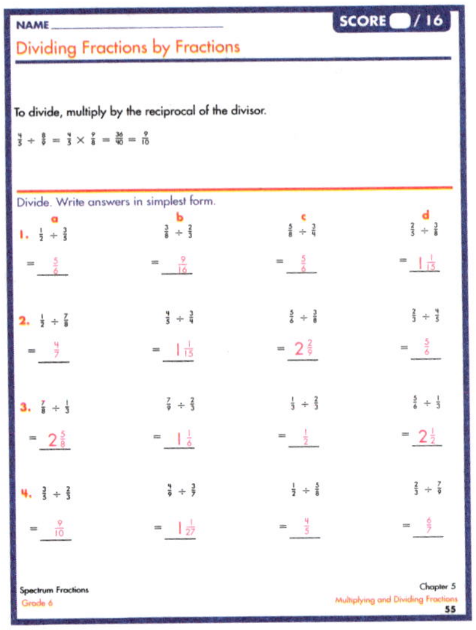

NAME

SCORE / 16

Dividing Fractions by Fractions

To divide, multiply by the reciprocal of the divisor.

Divide. Write answers in simplest form.

Spectrum Fractions
Grade 6

Chapter 5
Multiplying and Dividing Fractions
55

55

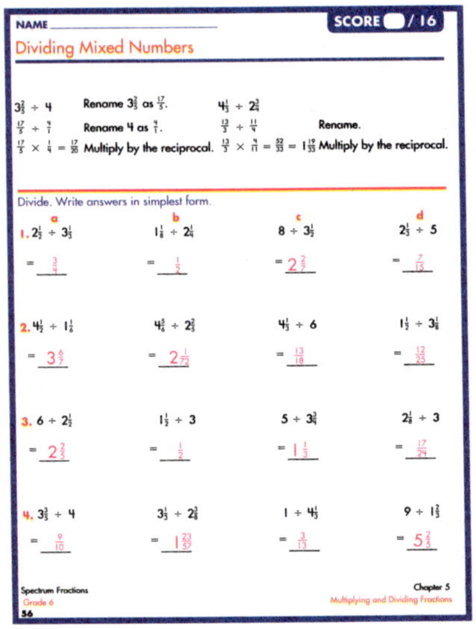

NAME

SCORE / 16

Dividing Mixed Numbers

Multiply by the reciprocal.

Divide. Write answers in simplest form.

Spectrum Fractions
Grade 6
56

Chapter 5
Multiplying and Dividing Fractions

56

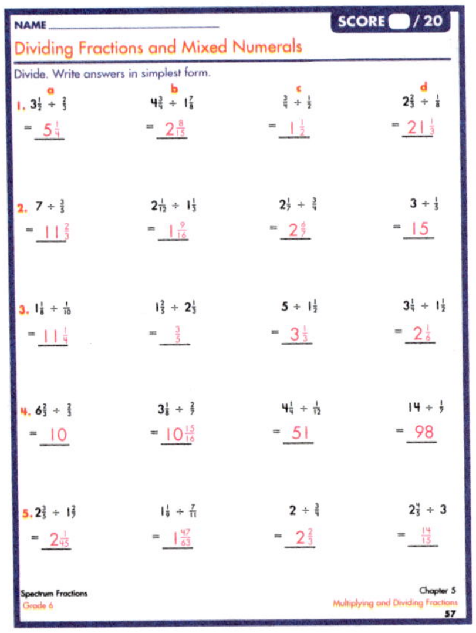

NAME

SCORE / 20

Dividing Fractions and Mixed Numerals

Divide. Write answers in simplest form.

Spectrum Fractions
Grade 6

Chapter 5
Multiplying and Dividing Fractions
57

57

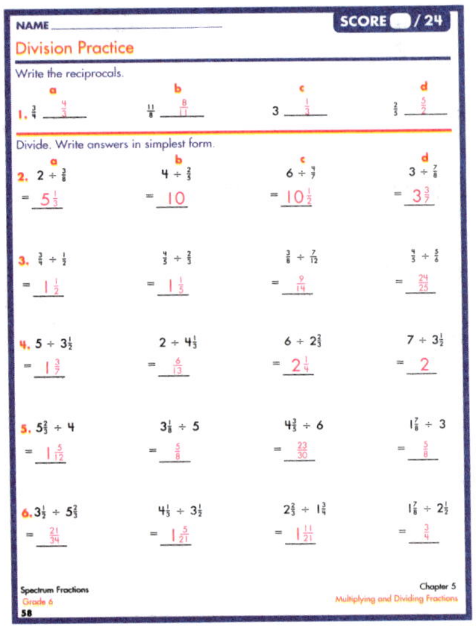

NAME

SCORE / 24

Division Practice

Write the reciprocals.

Divide. Write answers in simplest form.

Spectrum Fractions
Grade 6
58

Chapter 5
Multiplying and Dividing Fractions

58

Answer Key

Answer Key

Page 65 — Dividing Fractions by Fractions

1. $2\frac{1}{4}$ pieces
2. $1\frac{1}{2}$ pieces
3. $1\frac{1}{3}$ pieces

Page 66 — Dividing Whole Numbers and Fractions

1. $\frac{3}{2}$
2. $\frac{1}{6}$ yard
3. $\frac{1}{8}$ yard

Page 67 — Dividing Mixed Numbers

1. $2\frac{1}{2}$ containers
2. $2\frac{13}{20}$ containers
3. $1\frac{1}{4}$ pounds

Page 68 — Check What You Learned: Problem Solving: Multiplying and Dividing Fractions

1. $\frac{1}{6}$ of the garden
2. $2\frac{2}{3}$ pieces
3. $\frac{1}{12}$ yard
4. $8\frac{1}{3}$ hours

Page 69 — Check What You Know: Fractions and Decimals

1. a. 0.2   b. 0.23   c. 0.4   d. 0.75   e. 0.98
2. 0.6 = $\frac{3}{5}$; 0.08 = $\frac{2}{25}$; 2.25 = $2\frac{1}{4}$; 3.15 = $3\frac{3}{20}$; 2.2 = $2\frac{1}{5}$
3. a. 1.6   b. 2.25   c. 0.240
4. a. 2.5   b. 5.24   c. 2.046
5. a. 5.8   b. 1.35   c. 6.628
6. a. 6.2   b. 2.90   c. 3.720

Page 70 — Tenths and Hundredths

1. a. 0.3   b. 0.1   c. 0.07   d. 0.04
2. a. 2.4   b. 7.6   c. 21.02   d. 58.09
3. 0.4 = $\frac{2}{5}$; 0.8 = $\frac{4}{5}$; 0.06 = $\frac{3}{50}$; 0.39 = $\frac{39}{100}$
4. 9.6 = $9\frac{3}{5}$; 13.3 = $13\frac{3}{10}$; 11.16 = $11\frac{4}{25}$; 689.05 = $689\frac{1}{20}$
5. nine tenths 0.9; eight hundredths 0.08
6. five and two tenths 5.2; three and two hundredths 3.02
7. one tenth 0.1; seventy-three hundredths 0.73

Spectrum Fractions
Grade 6

Answer Key

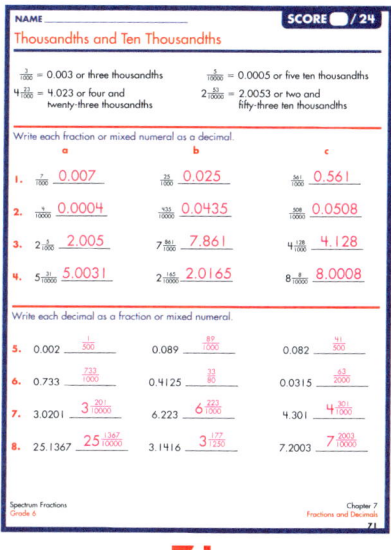

Answer Key

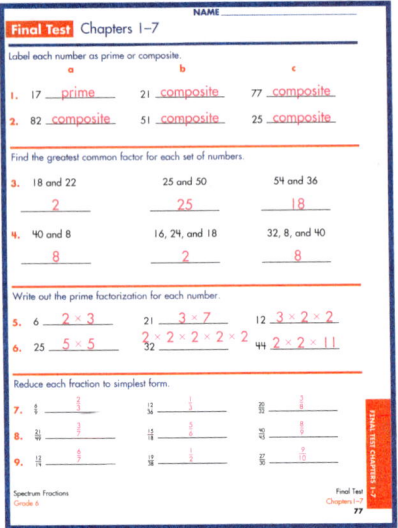